HEIDELBERG
CATECHISM

Other Small Town Theologian Books

The Belgic Confession: Truth Worth Dying For

Predestined for Joy: Finding Comfort in a Controversial Doctrine

Purchase Small Town Theologian books on Amazon (https://rb.gy/z0kocz) or head to wtsbooks.com.

Small Town Theologian Podcast & Blog

Biblical, confessional, and practical truth in 10 minutes or less. Recorded in Jonathan Shirk's walk-in closet, the Small Town Theologian podcast is a compact show bringing you comforting gospel truths from a confessional Reformed perspective to help you and your family navigate life's many challenges.

Listen to the show on Apple Podcasts, Podcast Addict, Spotify, and other listening platforms. Head to **www.smalltowntheologian.org** to read the transcripts of the podcast episodes and other short and helpful posts. Email Jonathan at smalltowntheologian@gmail.com.

The
HEIDELBERG
CATECHISM

TRUE COMFORT FOR LIFE & DEATH

ZACHARIAS URSINUS

At the center of the cover design there is a bear. Zacharias Ursinus' real name was
Zacharias Baer in German and Zacharias Ursus in Latin. Being a big man, Zacharias
lightheartedly referred to himself as Ursinus meaning "little bear." See "Who are
the Reformed: Zacharias Ursinus," August 17, 2016,
https://www.youtube.com/watch?v=1kv3gmrw21o&t=36s.

Frederick III's original 1563 preface to the Heidelberg Catechism is used by
permission. http://heidelberg-
catechism.s3.amazonaws.com/Original%20Preface%20of%20Heidelberg%20Cate
chism%20(1563).pdf.

This version of the Heidelberg Catechism is used by permission from the Standing
Committee for the Publication of the Book of Praise of the Canadian Reformed
Churches (CanRC). It has been lightly revised and edited (61—my instead of mine;
77—Scripture references moved to footnote; 92—ESV was used; 98—speechless
instead of dumb; 108—inside instead of within; 122-125, 127-128—usages of thee,
thou, thy, and wilt changed to you, your, and will). American English spellings were
used. Punctuation and capitalization differ at points. You can find the CanRC
version printed in their Book of Praise: Anglo-Genevan Psalter (bookofpraise.ca).

The versions of the Nicene and Athanasian Creeds are used by permission from
the United Reformed Churches in North America (urcna.org).

Scripture quotations are from the ESV® Bible (The Holy Bible, English Standard
Version®), copyright © 2001 by Crossway, a publishing ministry of Good News
Publishers. Used by permission. All rights reserved.

To the weak and weary on their journey
through the wilderness to eternal glory with Christ.
May the profound truths of this catechism give you
discernment, comfort, assurance, rest, and joy.

CONTENTS

INTRODUCTION: A BRIEF HISTORY

T he Heidelberg Catechism is the fourth most widely circulated book in history behind only the Bible, *The Imitation of Christ*, and *Pilgrim's Progress*.[1] It has been translated into numerous languages and has been and continues to be the statement of faith of millions of Christians. Aside from its rich Biblical and theological content, its spirit is warm, pastoral, and reassuring, and it provides edifying and encouraging devotional content for children and adults alike. This "book of comfort," as the Heidelberg Catechism is sometimes called, "remains the most widely used and warmly praised catechism of the Reformation."[2]

How is a catechism published in 1563 relevant and helpful for *you* today? The answer is found in the original intent of the catechism. The history of the Heidelberg Catechism provides helpful insight into the *original* and *ongoing* purpose and value of the work. So to a brief history, we shall turn.

HISTORY

In the 16th century, the Holy Roman (German) Empire was composed of many small territories or states.[3] Among the most prominent of those territories was the Electoral Palatinate.[4]

---

[1] Joel R. Beeke and Sinclair Ferguson, eds., *Reformed Confessions Harmonized with an Annotated Bibliography of Reformed Doctrinal Works* (Grand Rapids: Baker, 1999), x.
[2] Ibid.
[3] Lyle D. Bierma, "The Hiedleberg Catechism," © Ligonier Ministries, April 1, 2008, https://www.ligonier.org/learn/articles/heidelberg-catechism/.
[4] A *palatine* is an official who possesses judicial power delegated from a prince. A *palatinate* is the territory in which the *palatine* exercises his power.

This notable territory was divided into two parts: the Lower and Upper Palatinate. Nestled in the Lower Palatinate was the university town and capital city of Heidelberg.

Seven electors, who governed in the Holy Roman Empire and had great power and influence, had the joint responsibility of electing the Emperor. Charles V was Emperor from 1519–1556. He was the devout Roman Catholic Emperor who called Martin Luther to the Diet of Worms and strongly opposed the Reformation. Though hostility against Protestantism was great in the Empire, the Protestant cause was gaining traction in Heidelberg and other places, and Electors would play a vital role in Protestantism.

After defeating the Schmalkaldic League[5] in the Schmalkaldic War, enacting the Augsburg Interim,[6] and suppressing the ongoing Reformation, Charles V approved the Peace of Augsburg in 1555, a treaty which instilled peace between Roman Catholics and Lutherans and allowed each ruler to decide his territory's religion. Dr. N. R. Needham said the Peace of Augsburg "was a milestone in the history of religious toleration."[7] He added:

> It stipulated the "territorial principle", [sic] that a region was to follow the faith of its ruler . . . If anyone in a particular region disagreed with his ruler's religion, he was allowed to move to a different region . . . In any city where both Lutherans and Roman Catholics were represented, each was to be tolerated.[8]

---

[5] The Schmalkaldic League was an alliance of German Protestant princes who fought for religious freedom in the Holy Roman Empire.
[6] The Augsburg Interim was Charles V's imperial decree which essentially mandated Roman Catholicism.
[7] Dr. N. R. Needham, 2,000 Years of Christ's Power – Part Three: Renaissance and Reformation (London, England: Grace Publications Trust), 331.
[8] Ibid.

Despite the treaty's protection of religious liberty and Lutherans, it was problematic as it did not leave room for the Reformed faith in the Empire. Regardless of the opposition to Reformed thinking from the Roman Catholics and Lutherans, the Palatinate became a hotbed of the Reformed faith.[9]

Louis V was Elector in the Palatinate from 1508-1544. He was not interested in spiritual reform; he was more interested in politics and hunting.[10] He was succeeded by his brother, Frederick II, who served from 1544-1556 and was more favorable toward Protestantism. The Palatinate became Lutheran during Frederick II's rule. Otto Henry, a Lutheran, was his successor and ruled from 1556-1559. He served for only three years, yet he promoted Protestant catechesis and worship, established the Bibliotheca Palatina or "Palatinate library" in Heidelberg, and sent out a team to assess the spiritual condition of the churches in his territory. Sadly, the results of the spiritual assessment revealed that ministers were ill-equipped. Likewise, the people (including children and youth) were ignorant of Scripture and Christian doctrine and were therefore spiritually anemic, superstitious, and stuck in unhelpful traditions.[11]

Otto Henry progressed the Protestant cause in the Palatinate. However, he died in 1559. His nephew, Frederick III, succeeded him. With this change, the Reformed faith surged in the Palatinate (Frederick served until 1576).

Frederick was a sincere and godly man.[12] Though he grew up Roman Catholic and married a Lutheran, he would play an integral role in advancing the Reformed faith throughout the Palatinate and eventually the world.[13]

---

[9] Ibid., 340.
[10] Canadian Reformed Theological Seminary, "Reform in the Palatinate," http://www.heidelberg-catechism.com/en/history/.
[11] Ibid.
[12] Needham, 2,000 Years, 340.
[13] Ibid.

While Otto Henry was Elector, he had assembled a theologically diverse faculty at the University of Heidelberg (i.e. Lutheran, Reformed, Zwinglian).[14] There was theological tension and spiritual immaturity in the Palatinate and Heidelberg; "Frederick inherited a *religiously confused* Palatinate."[15]

Theological conflict necessitated Frederick to make a decisive move. So, in June of 1560, Frederick held a five-day disputation to discern the theological differences between the Lutherans and the Reformed. He sided with the Reformed. This led him to dismiss Tilemann Heshusius, who held Lutheran convictions and opposed Reformed theology, from his roles as professor of theology at the University of Heidelberg and preacher at the Church of the Holy Spirit in Heidelberg. This was an important turning point. The churches in Heidelberg and the Palatinate were in disrepair and needed revitalization or reformation, the University of Heidelberg was out a professor of theology, and the Church of the Holy Spirit needed a preacher! Frederick III was committed to reformation for the glory of God, so he made important decisions that would produce much spiritual fruit for years to come.

Back in 1556, Frederick III's teenage son, Herman, tried to cross the Auron River in France in a boat with some college friends. They all had been drinking. Caspar Olevianus, a twenty-year-old student, watched from the shore. Eventually, the boat capsized, and the young men began to drown. Olevianus jumped into the water to save his friend Herman but failed, and Herman drowned. Olevianus would have drowned as well, but Herman's servant, who mistook him for Herman,

---

[14] R. Scott Clark, "Introduction to the Heidelberg Catechism," Friday, August 30, 2013, https://heidelblog.net/2013/08/introduction-to-the-heidelberg-catechism/.
[15] Ibid., italics added.

saved Olevianus.[16] Simonetta Carr recounts, "In the fright of the moment, Olevianus promised God to serve him as preacher to the Germans if his life could be spared."[17] This promise was fulfilled when Frederick III, remembering Olevianus' attempt to save his son several years before, bailed him out of jail[18] and brought him to Heidelberg to teach and preach the Reformed faith. Olevianus served in the University of Heidelberg but eventually was replaced in order to focus primarily on preaching.

Frederick invited the well-known reformer, Peter Martyr Vermigli, to serve as professor of theology at the University, but he declined because of old age. Instead, he recommended a bright student of his, Zacharias Ursinus.[19] Ursinus accepted the position in 1561. This hire would put the city and the University of Heidelberg on the map as the origin of one of the most clear, compelling, and beautiful expressions of the Christian faith.

Frederick III understood that the Palatinate was not in good spiritual order. However, he also understood that the University of Heidelberg was now in much better theological hands. What could unify his territory in the Reformed faith? Frederick concluded a new catechism needed to be written and published. A Reformed catechism would provide theological clarity, harmony, and direction for the families, schools, and churches of the Palatinate. Frederick, sometimes called "Frederick the Pious," commissioned Zacharias Ursinus and Caspar Olevianus, the young professor of theology and court preacher, to prepare a catechism for the instruction of youth, guidance of pastors and teachers, and overall

---

[16] Simonetta Carr, "Caspar Olevianus and the Birthday Sermon that Split a Town in Half," Place for Truth, August 10, 2017, https://www.placefortruth.org/blog/caspar-olevianus-and-birthday-sermon-split-town-half.
[17] Ibid.
[18] Caspar Olevianus was emprisoned for boldly rebutting Roman Catholic doctrines and preaching the gospel in Trier, his hometown which was decidedly Roman Catholic.
[19] Needham, 2,000 Years, 341.

edification of Christians in the Palatinate.[20] This catechism became the Heidelberg Catechism.

The first draft of the Heidelberg Catechism was completed in 1562 and was revised by a synod and published in 1563 in Heidelberg. Ursinus and Olevianus were given oversight of the catechism. Though Ursinus was the primary author of the content, and Olevianus was closely involved (historians are unsure to what extent), the catechism was the product of the teamwork of brilliant theological minds who drew from various other significant theological works (these theologians helped with editing and gave final approval). Frederick himself wrote:

> With the advice and coöperation [sic] of our entire theological faculty in this place, and of all Superintendents and distinguished servants of the Church, we have secured preparation of a summary course of instruction or catechism of our Christian Religion, according to the word of God, in the German and Latin languages.[21]

Frederick was also involved and played a central role in the creation and distribution of the Heidelberg Catechism. Historian Dr. R. Scott Clark noted:

> The churches needed a clear, unambiguous articulation about what Scripture teaches concerning the most important questions of the Christian faith and life.[22]

The Heidelberg Catechism stands among the most organized, well-defined, beautiful, and helpful statements of the "faith

---

[20] Beeke and Ferguson, *Reformed Confessions*, ix.
[21] The original 1563 preface by Frederick III, http://heidelberg-catechism.s3.amazonaws.com/Original%20Preface%20of%20Heidelberg%20Catechism%20(1563).pdf.
[22] Clark, "Introduction to the Heidelberg Catechism."

that was once for all delivered to the saints" (Jude 3). Dr. Bierma rightly concludes:

> Like the others, it provides an explanation of the basic elements of the Christian faith: the Apostles' Creed, the Ten Commandments, the Lord's Prayer, and the sacraments. What is distinctive about the HC, however, is that it connects these explanations to a single over-arching theme, the theme of *comfort*.[23]

The 129 questions were helpfully organized in 52 sections or Lord's Days which parallel the weeks of the year and aim at giving readers *comfort*. The content and structure provided a well-organized and compelling curriculum for the ministers to use for their Sunday afternoon preaching through the year.[24]

The Heidelberg Catechism unified the Palatinate in the Reformed faith. It was used in churches and schools of the Palatinate to educate young and old alike and to ignite true spiritual reformation. It also began to spread throughout the world in diverse languages. Dr. Needham concludes:

> The Heidelberg Catechism became arguably the most important of all Reformed confessions, gaining acceptance across the entire Reformed world, especially in Germany and the Dutch Republic.[25]

It's important to note that the Heidelberg Catechism was not the brainchild of just one man or the statement of faith of a few. It articulates what millions of Christians believed in ages past and still believe today.

---

[23] Bierma, "The Hiedleberg Catechism," italics added.
[24] Ibid.
[25] Needham, 2,000 Years, 341.

RELEVANCE FOR TODAY

The spiritual and theological condition of evangelical Christianity in the United States is noticeably impaired. Since 2014, Ligonier Ministries and LifeWay Research have conducted a theological survey every other year. A quick glance at these surveys reveals that evangelicals need clarity and teaching on the essential doctrines of the Christian faith.[26]

Perhaps the group of people who need the Heidelberg Catechism the most is evangelical Christian parents and their children. When Elector Frederick III came to power, the youth in the Palatinate were suffering from the lack of proper instruction in the Christian faith. Frederick noticed that some youth were "entirely without Christian instruction." Others were "unsystematically taught." He concluded that many had "grown up without the fear of God and the knowledge of His word" and were "burdened with unsound doctrines." The people needed clear law and gospel teaching. The same is true for many children and youth in Christian families today; they simply have not been instructed well in the foundational truths of the Christian faith, and they desperately need law and gospel preaching and teaching.

In Ephesians 6:4, Paul exhorts fathers (and certainly mothers ought to do the same) to "bring [their children] up in the discipline and instruction of the Lord." Numerous Scriptures direct parents to teach their children the Christian faith.[27] Yet, many Christian parents do not have a well-defined plan to do this effectively. Sadly, many Christian parents didn't experience Ephesians 6:4 in their own families or observe it in other Christian families. Scores of parents grew up in homes

---

[26] "2020 State of American Theology Study," Ligonier Ministries & LifeWay Research, thestateoftheology.com.
[27] See Deut. 4:9; 6:4-9; 11:18-21; Ps. 78:1-8; Prov. 22:6; 2 Tim. 1:5; 3:15.

where church attendance was irregular and little to no attention was given to family worship and instruction at home. So, unaware of how to disciple their children effectively in the daily rhythms and demands of life, parents often continue the detrimental patterns of their childhoods.

The Heidelberg Catechism was created for the instruction of youth, guidance of ministers, and encouragement of Christians. The catechism proves a great resource for parents and churches. It charts a course for discipleship. The catechism amasses the most important doctrines of the Christian faith and organizes them into a logical and helpful framework (*guilt, grace, gratitude*). It's an excellent summary course of Christian doctrine and, because of its helpful structure, provides instructional material for the entire year.

The church in the United States is in desperate need of reformation, and the Heidelberg Catechism can help. As more parents follow the discipleship plan of the Heidelberg Catechism to instruct their children at home, and perhaps more ministers teach it to their congregations, by God's grace and Spirit, parents and churches will be better equipped to pass a robust understanding of the Christian faith onto the next generation. As the Spirit of God works, families and churches will also experience a deeper sense of comfort and joy in Christ and a renewed excitement for loving God and their neighbors.

HOW TO PROFIT MOST
FROM THE CATECHISM

T here have been many great drummers in history, but they didn't start out great. They became great by mastering the basics of rhythm: *whole notes, half notes, quarter notes, etc.* The most basic rhythms provided them the foundation for jaw-dropping beats.

The Christian life has a basic rhythm. This rhythm provides the structure for the beautiful music of God's comfort and joy in our lives. If this rhythm becomes irregular or we lose tempo, the beautiful sound of God's comfort and joy will not sound right to us. We do sometimes lose tempo, and when we do, we need to once again hear the divine metronome of the law and the gospel in Scripture. As we fall back into time, we can hear the beauty of God's comfort and joy once again. What's the rhythm of the Christian life? *Guilt, grace, gratitude.*

To *catechize* is to teach essential Biblical truths by using a question and answer format. A catechism is a collection of basic and crucial Christian truths presented in question and answer format. Good catechisms ask the most important questions and give helpful and applicable answers for the greater knowledge, wisdom, discernment, and comfort of learners.

The structure of the Heidelberg Catechism is important to understand in order to maximize its value. The first question and answer present our only comfort in life and death. The second follows by asking, "What do you need to know in order to live and die in the joy of this comfort?" The answer given is the outline for the entire catechism and the rhythm of the Christian life:

First, how great my sins and misery are; second, how I am delivered from all my sins and misery; third, how I am to be thankful to God for such deliverance.

There it is: *guilt, grace, gratitude*. Memorize that rhythm. Behind these three beats are the most significant truths you need to know in order to have true, profound, and enduring comfort and joy in life. The rhythm of *guilt, grace, gratitude* will not only help you understand the Bible but will also help you walk the road of sanctification by the Spirit.

First, the Heidelberg Catechism follows the structure of the book of Romans. Paul lays out *guilt* in chapters 1-3, *grace* in chapters 3-11, and *gratitude* in chapters 12-16.

The *guilt* section of the Heidelberg Catechism (Q&A 3-11), therefore, explains that God's law (or Ten Commandments) exposes our sin and misery. Only when we understand how we have broken God's law and deserve His just wrath and condemnation will we understand our deep need for Jesus Christ, the Savior of sinners.

The *grace* section (Q&A 12-85) explains how God delivers us from our sin and misery through the redemptive work of His Son Jesus Christ. Included in *grace* is an exposition of the Apostles' Creed and the sacraments of baptism and the Lord's Supper which, along with the preaching of God's Word, are means God uses to extend His grace to us.

The *gratitude* section (Q&A 86-129) explains how the Christian life is lived and how we are to express our love, devotion, and thankfulness to God. Included in *gratitude* is an exposition of the Ten Commandments and the Lord's Prayer, two portions of Scripture which clarify how we are to walk by the Spirit in love for God and our neighbors.

Second, the 129 questions are broken down into 52 Lord's Days or 52 subsections that align with the 52 weeks of the year. Every week of the year you can study and meditate on the heartening Biblical content of the corresponding Lord's Day. This provides space for repetition, memorization, and discussion, all of which foster a deeper understanding of the central doctrines of the Christian faith. This logical and helpful structure makes the Heidelberg Catechism a great resource for *regular* personal, family, and church worship.

FOR PARENTS & CHILDREN

Parents, this catechism is among the very best resources available to you to help you learn the Christian faith and teach it to your children. A regular pattern of family worship at home throughout the week is an opportunity to systematically learn rich and comforting truths as a family. Regular family worship could transform your family.

If daily family worship at home is not a consistent part of your lives, here is a simple way to get started. With a little prioritization and discipline, and of course God's grace and Spirit, you can do it. It is important to begin as soon as possible, even if you have infant children. Establishing a routine now will also establish family expectations and help you and your children for years to come. *The ideal is that your children grow up knowing nothing other than regular daily family worship.* And if you have older children, do not despair; it's never too late to start.

- **Prioritize daily family worship**. If you do not *truly* believe passages like Deuteronomy 6:4-9 and Ephesians 6:4, you will not commit yourself to discipling your kids at home, and family worship will never become the blessing it could be for your family. A successful routine of daily family worship begins with a conviction in your heart.
- **Discipline and routine are top priority**. Get started and do not stop. Many things will threaten your routine, so you must plan ahead. Treat family worship as an important appointment. The goal is to create the habit.

- **Choose the most convenient time and location**. What time works for your family? Breakfast, lunch, dinner, or bedtime? When does it work best for the entire family to gather together? If there is not a time your family can all be together, your family is probably too busy. You should probably remove some things from the calendar. Where in the house might be the most comfortable to meet?
- **Start with 10-15 minutes**. You can achieve much in ten minutes a day. You can always increase the minutes as the habit forms, but start small and experience some success first.
- **Choose a simple liturgy**. Only a few elements are necessary for meaningful family worship. Here are some suggestions:

  o *Opening prayer*. Begin by asking God for His grace, Spirit, and blessing.
  o *Catechization through repetition*. Whatever week of the year it is, study that Lord's Day in the HC. Or just work your way through the catechism at a pace that is right for your family. Repetition and review are very helpful. Parents should explain the content and help their children understand. It is best to aim the discussion at comprehension and application.
  o *Bible reading*. Choose a book of the Bible and read through it little by little taking a section at a time. Try to draw out one significant point from the passage. A great idea is to read and discuss the passage of Scripture your minister will be preaching the upcoming Sunday.
  o *Sharing prayer requests*. Share personal requests. Confess sin to one another. Pray for and encourage one another. Pray for your church, government, and community. Pray for unbelieving loved ones. Everyone should pray. Keep a prayer log. This is a great

opportunity for parents to pray for their children out loud.

An additional element you could add is **singing**. Sing psalms and Biblical hymns and choruses. Use a good psalter or hymnal. Musical family members can lead. Let the kids dance. Learning to sing Scripture and theologically rich songs together is very meaningful.

This may seem like a lot, but you may be surprised at the blessings and benefits that come from 10-15 minutes of focused family worship. If you trust the Lord to work in your family, and you commit yourself to faithful leadership, your investment in family worship will be worth it. Imagine how precious the gift of daily family worship will be for your children when they are 25. Just a little bit at a time can instill in your children a deep understanding of God's Word and the comfort and joy the gospel of Jesus Christ gives believers.

A great resource to help you begin family worship is the *Small Town Theologian* (smalltowntheologian.org) podcast. You can find the show on Apple Podcasts, Podcast Addict, Google Podcasts, and other apps. The series "Five Essential Gifts to Give Your Kids" explores the topic of parents disciplining their children and will help you get started (episodes 032-037).

There is no perfect way to do family worship. One size does not fit all. The important thing is to create the routine of gathering together to learn, discuss, apply, and delight in God's law and gospel every day.

FOR MINISTERS

Brothers, God has called you to preach and teach His people for their comfort, strength, growth, and joy. First Timothy 4:13 says, "devote yourself to the public reading of Scripture, to exhortation, to *teaching*." Second Timothy 4:2 adds, "preach the word; be ready in season and out of season; reprove, rebuke, and exhort, *with complete patience and teaching*." It is a high calling to *teach* God's people how to think about and apply God's Word.

It's possible for ministers of the gospel to preach and teach God's Word but fail to help their congregations connect the dots of Scripture. It is possible to teach a lot of wonderful truths without teaching the most important truths. How does a minister have balance in his preaching and teaching ministry? How does a minister preach the whole counsel of God (Acts 20:27)? How does a minister ensure that he is not trying to feed steak to infants who can't digest it (1 Cor. 3:2; Heb. 5:11-14)? The Heidelberg Catechism can bring balance.

One of the reasons the Heidelberg Catechism was written was to give guidance to ministers in what to teach their congregations. A skilled theological team worked together to produce the catechism in order to give ministers a carefully charted course of instruction for their people. By teaching the Biblical truths summarized in the catechism, ministers would give their congregations a balanced diet of law and gospel as well as a Biblical *guilt, grace, gratitude* rhythm for life and godliness. Ministers who train their people in the Biblical doctrine of the Heidelberg Catechism will be leading people toward knowledge, wisdom, discernment, and godliness.

Here are two encouragements for ministers. These two points are major factors in the ongoing reformation of the church in the United States and the world. If your church is plateaued or even dying, it's in great need of these things. As the Holy Spirit sovereignly works, these two things can bring you and your people increasing growth, strength, and comfort.

- **Devote yourself to heartfelt, passionate, and Christ-centered *expositional preaching* in *morning* worship services**.

People are hungry for God's Word, even if they do not realize it. They need to hear from God in the Scriptures to be transformed. Scripture is clear: "preach the word" (2 Tim. 4:2). As the Apostle Paul said:

> All Scripture is breathed out by God and profitable for teaching, for reproof, for correction, and for training in righteousness, that the man of God may be complete, equipped for every good work. (2 Tim. 3:16–17)

Though the world will not esteem God's *profitable* Word, it's God's divine pleasure to save everyone who believes the foolish message of Christ which we gladly preach (1 Cor. 1:21).

Christ-centered expositional preaching is honest preaching. It guides preachers through the topics God wants them to address, presents the centrality and supremacy of Christ, and protects ministers and congregations from the temptation to avoid certain topics. Christ-centered expositional preaching has accountability built into it. Devote yourself to fairly and faithfully preaching the law and gospel God has put in the text. Let the text of Scripture decide what you preach! Preach through books of the Bible and take time to unpack every verse (in some cases groups of verses) for the good of God's people. If you do this faithfully, God will use you to feed and grow His people.

- **Devote yourself to heartfelt, passionate, and Christ-centered *catechetical preaching* in *evening* worship services.**

Many churches no longer have an evening worship service. It would not be farfetched to say that the prevalence of Biblical illiteracy, theological confusion, and waning holiness in the church in the United States are, at least in part, the result of the disappearance of Sunday evening worship.

Have you and your elders considered how influential and helpful returning to the Reformational pattern of *morning and evening worship* could prove to be for your church? The benefits of an evening service (perhaps coupled with a fellowship meal), even if only a handful of people attend, could be transformational for you and your church.

The evening worship service is a wonderful opportunity to preach and teach through the Heidelberg Catechism. The catechism becomes the yearly preaching schedule. Allowing the catechism to guide your church through profound and essential Biblical texts and truths could be transformative. The Heidelberg Catechism is, in a sense, a type of sermon. It explains Scripture. Therefore, it acts as one large sermon outline that directs you through an entire year.

The impact of catechetical preaching on the church of the United States would be immense if ministers like you committed themselves to doing it in an afternoon or evening worship service. This kind of preaching, connected to expositional preaching, would provide theological unity, constancy, and vigor. Because the Heidelberg Catechism is so focused on *comfort* in Christ, preaching through the catechism would also encourage the congregation to connect the dots of Scripture for their own comfort and joy.

So, as a minster, consider the original purpose of the Heidelberg Catechism. Consider why Frederick III commissioned it. Consider the impact it has had in Germany, the Dutch Republic, and the world from the 16th century up until today. Then ask yourself, "Does this 16th century catechism have something to offer me and my church?" The deeper you delve into the comfort of this catechism, the deeper and more helpful your preaching ministry will become, that is, if you trust the sovereign grace and Spirit of our Lord Jesus Christ to continually transform you and the flock entrusted to your care.

ELECTOR FREDERICK III'S PREFACE TO THE HC (1563)

W e, Frederic [sic], Archcarver and Elector of the Holy Roman Empire, Duke in Bavaria, by the grace of God, Elector Palatine on the Rhine, &c., present to all and each of our Superintendents, Pastors, Preachers, Officers of the Church, and Schoolmasters, throughout our Electorate of the Rhenish Palatinate, our grace and greeting, and do them, herewith, to wit:

Inasmuch as we acknowledge that we are bound by the admonition of the Divine word, and also by natural duty and relation, and have finally determined to order and administer our office, calling, and government, not only for the promotion and maintenance of quiet and peaceable living, and for the support of upright and virtuous walk and conversation among our subjects, but also and above all, constantly to admonish and lead them to devout knowledge and fear of the Almighty and His holy word of salvation, as the only foundation of all virtue and obedience, and to spare no pains, so far as in us lies, with all sincerity to promote their temporal and eternal welfare, and to contribute to the defence [sic] and maintenance of the same:

And, although apprised on entering upon our government, how our dear cousins and predecessors, Counts Palantine, Electors, &c, of noble and blessed memory, have instituted and proposed divers Christian and profitable measures and appliances for the furtherance of the glory of God and the upholding of civil discipline and order:

Notwithstanding this purpose was not in every respect prosecuted with the appropriate zeal, and the expected and desired fruit did not accrue therefrom—we are now induced not only to renew the same, but also, as the exigencies of the times demand, to improve, reform, and further to establish them. Therefore we also have ascertained that by no means the least defect of our system is found in the fact, that our blooming youth is disposed to be careless in respect to Christian doctrine, both in the schools and churches of our principality—some, indeed, being entirely without Christian instruction, others being unsystematically taught, without any established, certain, and clear catechism, but merely according to individual plan or judgment; from which, among other great defects, the consequence has ensued, that they have, in too many instances, grown up without the fear of God and the knowledge of His word, having enjoyed no profitable instruction, or otherwise have been perplexed with irrelevant and needless questions, and at times have been burdened with unsound doctrines.

And now, whereas both temporal and spiritual offices, government and family discipline, cannot otherwise be maintained—and in order that discipline and obedience to authority and all other virtures [sic] may increase and be multiplied among subjects—it is essential that our youth be trained in early life, and above all, in the pure and consistent doctrine of the holy Gospel, and be well exercised in the proper and true knowledge of God:

Therefore, we have regarded it as a high obligation, and as the most important duty of our government, to give attention to this matter, to do away with this defect, and to introduce the needful improvements:

And accordingly, with the advice and coöperation [sic] of our entire theological faculty in this place, and of all Superintendents and distinguished servants of the Church, we have secured preparation of a summary course of instruction or catechism of our Christian Religion, according to the word of God, in the German and Latin languages; in order not only that the youth in churches and schools may be piously instructed in such Christian doctrine, and be thoroughly trained therein, but also that the Pastors and Schoolmasters themselves may be provided with a fixed form and model, by which to regulate the instruction of youth, and not, at their option, adopt daily changes, or introduce erroneous doctrine:

We do herewith affectionately admonish and enjoin upon every one of you, that you do, for the honour [sic] of God and our subjects, and also for the sake of your own soul's profit and welfare, thankfully accept this proffered Catechism or course of instruction, and that you do diligently and faithfully represent and explain the same according to its true import, to the youth in our schools and churches, and also from the pulpit to the common people, that you teach, and act, and live in accordance with it, in the assured hope, that if our youth in early life are earnestly instructed and educated in the word of God, it will please Almighty God also to grant reformation of public and private morals, and temporal and eternal welfare. Desiring, as above said, that all this may be accomplished, we have made this provision.

"Given at Heidelberg, Tuesday, the nineteenth of January, in the year 1563 after the birth of Christ, our dear Lord and Saviour [sic]."

THE HEIDELBERG CATECHISM

SUMMARY: YOUR ONLY COMFORT

LORD'S DAY 1

Q. 1. What is your only comfort in life and death?

A. That I am not my own,[1] but belong with body and soul, both in life and in death,[2] to my faithful Savior Jesus Christ.[3] He has fully paid for all my sins with His precious blood[4] and has set me free from all the power of the devil.[5] He also preserves me in such a way[6] that without the will of my heavenly Father not a hair can fall from my head;[7] indeed, all things must work together for my salvation.[8] Therefore, by His Holy Spirit, He also assures me of eternal life[9] and makes me heartily willing and ready from now on to live for Him.[10]

[1] 1 Cor. 6:19–20 [2] Rom. 14:7-9 [3] 1 Cor. 3:23; Titus 2:14 [4] 1 Pet. 1:18–19; 1 John 1:7; 2:2 [5] John 8:34–36; Heb. 2:14–15; 1 John 3:8 [6] John 6:39–40; 10:27–30; 2 Thess. 3:3; 1 Pet. 1:5 [7] Matt. 10:29–31; Luke 21:16–18 [8] Rom. 8:28 [9] Rom. 8:15–16; 2 Cor. 1:21–22; 5:5; Eph. 1:13–14 [10] Rom. 8:14

Q. 2. What do you need to know in order to live and die in the joy of this comfort?

A. First, how great my sins and misery are;[1] second, how I am delivered from all my sins and misery;[2] third, how I am to be thankful to God for such deliverance.[3]

[1] Rom. 3:9-10; 1 John 1:10 [2] John 17:3; Acts 4:12; 10:43 [3] Matt. 5:16; Rom. 6:13; Eph. 5:8-10; 1 Pet. 2:9-10

GUILT: YOUR SIN & MISERY

LORD'S DAY 2

Q. 3. From where do you know your sins and misery?

A. From the law of God.[1]

[1] Rom. 3:20; 7:7-25

Q. 4. What does God's law require of us?

A. Christ teaches us this in a summary in Matthew 22: "You shall love the LORD your God with all your heart and with all your soul and with all your mind.[1] This is the great and first commandment. And a second is like it: You shall love your neighbor as yourself. On these two commandments depend all the Law and the prophets."[2]

[1] Deut. 6:5 [2] Lev. 19:18

Q. 5. Can you keep all this perfectly?

A. No,[1] I am inclined by nature to hate God and my neighbor.[2]

[1] Rom. 3:10, 23; 1 John 1:8, 10 [2] Gen. 6:5; 8:21; Jer. 17:9; Rom. 7:23; 8:7; Eph. 2:3; Titus 3:3

LORD'S DAY 3

Q. 6. Did God, then, create man so wicked and perverse?

A. No, on the contrary, God created man good[1] and in His image,[2] that is, in true righteousness and holiness,[3] so that he might rightly know God his Creator,[4] heartily love Him, and live with Him in eternal blessedness to praise and glorify Him.[5]

[1] Gen. 1:31 [2] Gen. 1:26-27 [3] Eph. 4:24 [4] Col. 3:10 [5] Ps. 8

Q. 7. From where, then, did man's depraved nature come?

A. From the fall and disobedience of our first parents, Adam and Eve, in Paradise,[1] for there our nature became so corrupt[2] that we are all conceived and born in sin.[3]

[1] Gen. 3 [2] Rom. 5:12, 18, 19 [3] Ps. 51:5

Q. 8. But are we so corrupt that we are totally unable to do any good and inclined to all evil?

A. Yes,[1] unless we are regenerated by the Spirit of God.[2]

[1] Gen. 6:5; 8:21; Job 14:4; Is. 53:6 [2] John 3:3-5

Q. 9. Is God, then, not unjust by requiring in His law what man cannot do?

A. No, for God so created man that he was able to do it.[1] But man, at the instigation of the devil[2] in deliberate disobedience,[3] robbed himself and all his descendants of these gifts.[4]

[1] Gen. 1:31 [2] Gen. 3:13; John 8:44; 1 Tim. 2:13-14 [3] Gen. 3:6 [4] Rom. 5:12, 18-19

Q. 10. Will God allow such disobedience and apostasy to go unpunished?

A. Certainly not. He is terribly displeased with our original sin as well as our actual sins. Therefore, He will punish them by a just judgment both now and eternally,[1] as He has declared: *"Cursed be everyone who does not abide by all things written in the Book of the Law, and do them."*[2]

[1] Gen. 2:17; Ex. 34:7; Ps. 5:4-6; 7:11; Nah. 1:2; Rom. 1:18; 5:12; Eph. 5:6; Heb. 9:27 [2] Deut. 27:26; Gal. 3:10

Q. 11. But is God not also merciful?

A. God is indeed merciful,[1] but He is also just.[2] His justice requires that sin committed against the most high majesty of God also be punished with the most severe, that is, with everlasting punishment of body and soul.[3]

[1] Ex. 20:6; 34:6-7; Ps. 103:8-9 [2] Ex. 20:5; 34:7; Deut. 7:9-11; Ps. 5:4-6; Heb. 10:30-31 [3] Matt. 25:45-46

GRACE: YOUR SALVATION IN CHRIST

LORD'S DAY 5

Q. 12. Since according to God's righteous judgment we deserve temporal and eternal punishment, how can we escape this punishment and be again received into favor?

A. God demands that His justice be satisfied.[1] Therefore, full payment must be made either by ourselves or by another.[2]

[1] Ex. 20:5; 23:7; Rom. 2:1-11 [2] Is. 53:11; Rom. 8:3-4

Q. 13. Can we ourselves make this payment?

A. Certainly not. On the contrary, we daily increase our debt.[1]

[1] Ps. 130:3; Matt. 6:12; Rom. 2:4-5

Q. 14. Can any mere creature pay for us?

A. No. In the first place, God will not punish another creature for the sin which man has committed.[1] Furthermore, no mere creature can sustain the burden of God's eternal wrath against sin and deliver others from it.[2]

[1] Ezek. 18:4, 20; Heb. 2:14-18 [2] Ps. 130:3; Nah. 1:6

Q. 15. What kind of mediator and deliverer must we seek?

A. One who is a true[1] and righteous[2] man and yet more powerful than all creatures; that is, one who is at the same time true God.[3]

[1] 1 Cor. 15:21; Heb. 2:17 [2] Is. 53:9; 2 Cor. 5:21; Heb. 7:26 [3] Is. 7:14; 9:6; Jer. 23:6; John 1:1; Rom. 8:3-4

LORD'S DAY 6

Q. 16. Why must He be a true and righteous man?

A. He must be a true man because the justice of God requires that the same human nature which has sinned should pay for sin.[1] He must be a righteous man because one who himself is a sinner cannot pay for others.[2]

[1] Rom: 5:12, 15; 1 Cor. 15:21; Heb. 2:14-16 [2] Heb. 7:26-27; 1 Pet. 3:18

Q. 17. Why must He at the same time be true God?

A. He must be true God so that by the power of His divine nature[1] He might bear in His human nature the burden of God's wrath[2] and might obtain for us and restore to us righteousness and life.[3]

[1] Is. 9:6 [2] Deut. 4:24; Nah. 1:6; Ps. 130:3 [3] Is. 53:5, 11; John 3:16; 2 Cor. 5:21

Q. 18. But who is that Mediator who at the same time is true God and a true and righteous man?

A. Our Lord Jesus Christ[1] whom God made our wisdom, our righteousness, and sanctification and redemption.[2]

[1] Matt. 1:21-23; Luke 2:11; 1 Tim. 2:5; 3:16 [2] 1 Cor. 1:30

Q. 19. From where do you know this?

A. From the holy gospel which God Himself first revealed in Paradise.[1] Later, He had it proclaimed by the patriarchs[2] and prophets[3] and foreshadowed by the sacrifices and other ceremonies of the law.[4] Finally, He had it fulfilled through His only Son.[5]

[1] Gen. 3:15 [2] Gen. 12:3; 22:18; 49:10 [3] Is. 53; Jer. 23:5-6; Mic. 7:18-20; Acts 10:43; Heb. 1:1 [4] Lev. 1-7; John 5:46; Heb. 10:1-10 [5] Rom. 10:4; Gal. 4:4-5; Col. 2:17

LORD'S DAY 7

Q. 20. Are all men, then, saved by Christ just as they perished through Adam?

A. No. Only those are saved who by a true faith are grafted into Christ and accept all His benefits.[1]

[1] Matt. 7:14; John 1:12; 3:16, 18, 36; Rom. 11:16-21

Q. 21. What is true faith?

A. True faith is a sure knowledge whereby I accept as true all that God has revealed to us in His Word.[1] At the same time, it is a firm confidence[2] that not only to others but also to me,[3]

God has granted forgiveness of sins, everlasting righteousness, and salvation,[4] out of mere grace, only for the sake of Christ's merits.[5] This faith the Holy Spirit works in my heart by the gospel.[6]

[1] John 17:3, 17; Heb. 11:1-3; James 2:19 [2] Rom. 4:18-21; 5:1; 10:10; Heb. 4:16 [3] Gal. 2:20 [4] Rom. 1:17; Heb. 10:10 [5] Rom. 3:20-26; Gal. 2:16; Eph. 2:8-10 [6] Acts 16:14; Rom. 1:16; 10:17; 1 Cor. 1:21

Q. 22. What, then, must a Christian believe?

A. All that is promised us in the Gospel[1] which the articles of our catholic and undoubted Christian faith teach us in a summary.

[1] Matt. 28:19; John 20:30-31

Q. 23. What are these articles?

A. I believe in God the Father almighty, Creator of heaven and earth. I believe in Jesus Christ, His only begotten Son, our Lord; He was conceived by the Holy Spirit, born of the virgin Mary; suffered under Pontius Pilate, was crucified, dead, and buried; He descended into hell; on the third day he arose from the dead; He ascended into heaven and sits at the right hand of God the Father almighty; from there He will come to judge the living and the dead. I believe in the Holy Spirit; I believe a holy catholic Christian church, the communion of saints; the forgiveness of sins; the resurrection of the body; and the life everlasting.

LORD'S DAY 8

Q. 24. How are these articles divided?

A. Into three parts: the first is about God the Father and our creation; the second about God the Son and our redemption; the third about God the Holy Spirit and our sanctification.

Q. 25. Since there is only one God,[1] why do you speak of three persons, Father, Son, and Holy Spirit?

A. Because God has so revealed Himself in His Word[2] that these three distinct persons are the one, true, eternal God.

[1] Deut. 6:4; Is. 44:6; 45:5; 1 Cor. 8:4, 6 [2] Gen. 1:2-3; Is. 61:1; 63:8-10; Matt. 3:16-17; 28:18-19; Luke 4:18; John 14:26; 15:26; 2 Cor. 13:14; Gal. 4:6; Titus 3:5-6

LORD'S DAY 9

Q. 26. What do you believe when you say "I believe in God the Father almighty, Creator of heaven and earth"?

A. That the eternal Father of our Lord Jesus Christ, who out of nothing created heaven and earth and all that is in them,[1] and who still upholds and governs them by His eternal counsel and providence,[2] is, for the sake of Christ His Son, my God and my Father.[3] In Him I trust so completely as to have no doubt that He will provide me with all things necessary for body and soul[4] and will also turn to my good whatever adversity He sends me in this life of sorrow.[5] He is able to do so as almighty God[6] and willing also as a faithful Father.[7]

[1] Gen. 1 and 2; Ex. 20:11; Job 38 and 39; Ps. 33:6; Is. 44:24; Acts 4:24; 14:15 [2] Ps. 104:27-30; Matt. 6:30; 10:29; Eph. 1:11 [3] John 1:12-13; Rom. 8:15-16; Gal. 4:4-7; Eph. 1:5 [4] Ps. 55:22; Matt. 6:25-26; Luke 12:22-31 [5] Rom. 8:28 [6] Gen. 18:14; Rom. 8:31-39 [7] Matt. 6:32-33; 7:9-11

LORD'S DAY 10

Q. 27. What do you understand by the providence of God?

A. God's providence is His almighty and ever-present power,[1] whereby, as with His hand, He still upholds heaven and earth and all creatures[2] and so governs them that leaf and blade, rain and drought, fruitful and barren years, food and drink, health and sickness, riches and poverty,[3] indeed, all things come not by chance[4] but by His fatherly hand.[5]

[1] Jer. 23:23-24; Acts 17:24-28 [2] Heb. 1:3 [3] Jer. 5:24; Acts 14:15-17; John 9:3; Prov. 22:2 [4] Prov. 16:33 [5] Matt. 10:29

Q. 28. What does it benefit us to know that God has created all things and still upholds them by His providence?

A. We can be patient in adversity,[1] thankful in prosperity,[2] and with a view to the future we can have a firm confidence in our faithful God and Father that no creature shall separate us from His love;[3] for all creatures are so completely in His hand that without His will they cannot so much as move.[4]

[1] Job. 1:21–22; Ps. 39:10; James 1:3 [2] Deut. 8:10; 1 Thess. 5:18 [3] Ps. 55:22; Rom. 5:3-5; 8:38-39 [4] Job 1:12; 2:6; Prov. 21:1; Acts 17:24-28

LORD'S DAY 11

Q. 29. Why is the Son of God called "Jesus," that is, "Savior"?

A. Because He saves us from all our sins,[1] and because salvation is not to be sought or found in anyone else.[2]

[1] Matt. 1:21; Heb. 7:25 [2] Is. 43:11; John 15:4-5; Acts 4:11-12; 1 Tim. 2:5

Q. 30. Do those believe in the only Savior Jesus who seek their salvation and well-being from saints, in themselves, or anywhere else?

A. No. Though they boast of Him in words, they in fact deny the only Savior Jesus.[1] For one of two things must be true: either Jesus is not a complete Savior or those who by true faith accept this Savior must find in Him all that is necessary for their salvation.[2]

[1] 1 Cor. 1:12-13; Gal. 5:4 [2] Col. 1:19-20; 2:10; 1 John 1:7

LORD'S DAY 12

Q. 31. Why is He called "Christ," that is, "Anointed"?

A. Because He has been ordained by God the Father and anointed with the Holy Spirit[1] to be our chief Prophet and Teacher,[2] who has fully revealed to us the secret counsel and will of God concerning our redemption;[3] our only High Priest,[4] who by the one sacrifice of His body has redeemed us,[5] and who continually intercedes for us before the Father;[6] and our eternal King,[7] who governs us by his Word and Spirit, and who defends and preserves us in the redemption obtained for us.[8]

[1] Ps. 45:7; Heb. 1:9; Is. 61:1; Luke 4:18; Luke 3:21-22 [2] Deut. 18:15; Acts 3:22 [3] John 1:18; 15:15 [4] Ps. 110:4; Heb. 7:17 [5] Heb. 9:12; 10:11-14 [6] Rom. 8:34; Heb. 9:24; 1 John 2:1 [7] Zach. 9:9; Matt. 21:5; Luke 1:33 [8] Matt. 28:18-20; John 10:28; Rev. 12:10-11

Q. 32. Why are you called a Christian?

A. Because I am a member of Christ by faith[1] and thus share in His anointing[2] so that I may as prophet confess His Name,[3] as priest present myself a living sacrifice of thankfulness to Him,[4] and as king fight with a free and good conscience against sin and the devil in this life[5] and hereafter reign with him eternally over all creatures.[6]

[1] 1 Cor. 12:12-27 [2] Joel 2:28; Acts 2:17; 1 John 2:27 [3] Matt. 10:32; Rom 10:9-10; Heb. 13:15 [4] Rom. 12:1; 1 Pet. 2:5, 9 [5] Gal. 5:16-17; Eph. 6:11; 1 Tim. 1:18-19 [6] Matt. 25:34; 2 Tim. 2:12

LORD'S DAY 13

Q. 33. Why is He called God's "only begotten Son," since we also are children of God?

A. Because Christ alone is the eternal, natural Son of God.[1] We, however, are children of God by adoption through grace for Christ's sake.[2]

[1] John 1:1-3, 14, 18; 3:16; Rom. 8:32; Heb. 1; 1 John 4:9 [2] John 1:12; Rom. 8:14-17; Gal. 4:6; Eph. 1:5-6

Q. 34. Why do you call him "our Lord"?

A. Because He has ransomed us, body and soul,[1] from all our sins, not with silver or gold but with His precious blood[2] and has freed us from all the power of the devil to make us His own possession.[3]

[1] 1 Cor. 6:20; 1 Tim. 2:5-6 [2] 1 Pet. 1:18-19 [3] Col. 1:13-14; Heb. 2:14-15

LORD'S DAY 14

Q. 35. What do you confess when you say "He was conceived by the Holy Spirit, born of the virgin Mary"?

A. The eternal Son of God, who is and remains true and eternal God,[1] took upon Himself a true human nature from the flesh and blood of the virgin Mary[2] through the working of the Holy Spirit.[3] Thus He is also the true seed of David[4] and like his brothers in every respect,[5] yet without sin.[6]

[1] John 1:1; 10:30-36; Rom. 1:3; 9:5; Col. 1:15-17; 1 John 5:20 [2] Matt. 1:18-23; John 1:14; Gal. 4:4; Heb. 2:14 [3] Luke 1:35 [4] 2 Sam. 7:12-16; Ps. 132:11; Matt. 1:1; Luke 1:32; Rom. 1:3 [5] Phil. 2:7; Heb. 2:17 [6] Heb. 4:15; 7:26-27

Q. 36. What benefit do you receive from the holy conception and birth of Christ?

A. He is our Mediator,[1] and with his innocence and perfect holiness covers, in the sight of God, my sin, in which I was conceived and born.[2]

[1] 1 Tim. 2:5-6; Heb. 9:13-15 [2] Rom. 8:3-4; 2 Cor. 5:21; Gal. 4:4-5; 1 Pet. 1:18-19

Q. 37. What do you confess when you say that He "suffered"?

A. During all the time He lived on earth, but especially at the end, Christ bore in body and soul the wrath of God against the sin of the whole human race.[1] Thus, by His suffering, as the only atoning sacrifice,[2] He has redeemed our body and soul from everlasting damnation[3] and obtained for us the grace of God, righteousness, and eternal life.[4]

[1] Is. 53; 1 Tim. 2:6; 1 Pet. 2:24; 3:18 [2] Rom. 3:25; 1 Cor. 5:7; Eph. 5:2; Heb. 10:14; 1 John 2:2; 4:10 [3] Rom. 8:1-4; Gal. 3:13; Col. 1:13; Heb. 9:12; 1 Pet. 1:18-19 [4] John 3:16; Rom. 3:24-26; 2 Cor. 5:21; Heb. 9:15

Q. 38. Why did he suffer "under Pontius Pilate" as judge?

A. Though innocent, Christ was condemned by an earthly judge,[1] and so He freed us from the severe judgment of God that was to fall on us.[2]

[1] Luke 23:13-24; John 19:4, 12-16 [2] Is. 53:4-5; 2 Cor. 5:21; Gal. 3:13

Q. 39. Does it have a special meaning that Christ was "crucified" and did not die in a different way?

A. Yes. Thereby I am assured that He took upon himself the curse which lay on me, for a crucified one was cursed by God.[1]

[1] Deut. 21:23; Gal. 3:13

Q. 40. Why was it necessary for Christ to humble himself even unto death?

A. Because of the justice and truth of God,[1] satisfaction for our sins could be made in no other way than by the death of the Son of God.[2]

[1] Gen. 2:17 [2] Rom. 8:3; Phil. 2:8; Heb. 2:9, 14–15

Q. 41. Why was he "buried"?

A. His burial testified that He had really died.[1]

[1] Is. 53:9; John 19:38-42; Acts 13:29; 1 Cor. 15:3-4

Q. 42. Since Christ has died for us, why do we still have to die?

A. Our death is not a payment for our sins, but it puts an end to sin and is an entrance into eternal life.[1]

[1] John 5:24; Phil. 1:21-23; 1 Thess. 5:9-10

Q. 43. What further benefit do we receive from Christ's sacrifice and death on the cross?

A. Through Christ's death, our old nature is crucified, put to death, and buried with Him[1] so that the evil desires of the flesh may no longer reign in us,[2] but that we may offer ourselves to Him as a sacrifice of thankfulness.[3]

[1] Rom. 6:5-11; Col. 2:11-12 [2] Rom. 6:12-14 [3] Rom. 12:1; Eph. 5:1-2

Q. 44. Why is there added, "He descended into hell"?

A. In my greatest sorrows and temptations, I may be assured and comforted that my Lord Jesus Christ, by His unspeakable anguish, pain, terror, and agony, which he endured throughout all His sufferings[1] but especially on the cross, has delivered me from the anguish and torment of hell.[2]

[1] Ps. 18:5-6; 116:3; Matt. 26:36-46; 27:45-46; Heb. 5:7-10 [2] Is. 53

LORD'S DAY 17

Q. 45. How does Christ's resurrection benefit us?

A. First, by His resurrection, He has overcome death, so that He could make us share in the righteousness which He had obtained for us by His death.[1] Second, by His power, we too are raised up to a new life.[2] Third, Christ's resurrection is to us a sure pledge of our glorious resurrection.[3]

[1] Rom. 4:25; 1 Cor. 15:16-20; 1 Pet. 1:3-5 [2] Rom. 6:5-11; Eph. 2:4-6; Col. 3:1-4 [3] Rom. 8:11; 1 Cor. 15:12-23; Phil. 3:20-21

LORD'S DAY 18

Q. 46. What do you confess when you say "He ascended into heaven"?

A. That Christ, before the eyes of His disciples, was taken up from the earth into heaven,[1] and that He is there for our benefit[2] until He comes again to judge the living and the dead.[3]

[1] Mark 16:19; Luke 24:50-51; Acts 1:9-11 [2] Rom. 8:34; Heb. 4:14; 7:23-25; 9:24 [3] Matt. 24:30; Acts 1:11

Q. 47. Is Christ, then, not with us until the end of the world as He has promised us?[1]

A. Christ is true man and true God. With respect to His human nature, He is no longer on earth,[2] but with respect to His divinity, majesty, grace, and Spirit, He is never absent from us.[3]

[1] Matt. 28:20 [2] Matt. 26:11; John 16:28; 17:11; Acts 3:19-21; Heb. 8:4 [3] Matt. 28:18-20; John 14:16-19; 16:13

Q. 48. But are the two natures in Christ not separated from each other if His human nature is not present wherever His divinity is?

A. Not at all, for His divinity has no limits and is present everywhere.[1] So it must follow that His divinity is indeed beyond the human nature which He has taken on and nevertheless is within this human nature and remains personally united with it.[2]

[1] Jer. 23:23, 24; Acts 7:48-49 [2] John 1:14; 3:13; Col. 2:9

Q. 49. How does Christ's ascension into heaven benefit us?

A. First, He is our advocate in heaven before His Father.[1] Second, we have our flesh in heaven as a sure pledge that He, our Head, will also take us, His members, up to Himself.[2] Third, He sends us His Spirit as a counter-pledge,[3] by whose power we seek the things that are above, where Christ is, seated at the right hand of God, and not the things that are on earth.[4]

[1] Rom. 8:34; 1 John 2:1 [2] John 14:2; 17:24; Eph. 2:4-6 [3] John 14:16; Acts 2:33; 2 Cor. 1:21-22; 5:5 [4] Col. 3:1-4

LORD'S DAY 19

Q. 50. Why is it added, "and sits at the right hand of God"?

A. Christ ascended into heaven to manifest Himself there as Head of His Church,[1] through whom the Father governs all things.[2]

[1] Eph. 1:20-23; Col. 1:18 [2] Matt. 28:18; John 5:22-23

Q. 51. How does the glory of Christ, our Head, benefit us?

A. First, by His Holy Spirit, He pours out heavenly gifts upon us, His members.[1] Second, by His power He defends and preserves us against all enemies.[2]

[1] Acts 2:33; Eph. 4:7-12 [2] Ps. 2:9; 110:1-2; John 10:27-30; Rev. 19:11-16

Q. 52. What comfort is it to you that Christ will "come to judge the living and the dead"?

A. In all my sorrow and persecution, I lift up my head and eagerly await as judge from heaven the very same person who before has submitted Himself to the judgment of God for my sake and has removed all the curse from me.[1] He will cast all His and my enemies into everlasting condemnation, but He will take me and all His chosen ones to Himself into heavenly joy and glory.[2]

[1] Luke 21:28; Rom. 8:22-25; Phil. 3:20-21; Titus 2:13-14 [2] Matt. 25:31-46; 1 Thess. 4:16-17; 2 Thess. 1:6-10

LORD'S DAY 20

Q. 53. What do you believe concerning "the Holy Spirit"?

A. First, He is, together with the Father and the Son, true and eternal God.[1] Second, He is also given to me[2] to make me by true faith share in Christ and all His benefits,[3] to comfort me,[4] and to remain with me forever.[5]

[1] Gen. 1:1-2; Matt. 28:19; Acts 5:3-4; 1 Cor. 3:16 [2] 1 Cor. 6:19; 2 Cor. 1:21-22; Gal. 4:6; Eph. 1:13 [3] Gal. 3:14; 1 Pet. 1:2 [4] John 15:26; Acts 9:31 [5] John 14:16-17; 1 Pet. 4:14

LORD'S DAY 21

Q. 54. What do you believe concerning "the holy catholic Christian church"?

A. I believe that the Son of God,[1] out of the whole human race,[2] from the beginning of the world to its end,[3] gathers, defends, and preserves for Himself,[4] by His Spirit and Word,[5] in the unity of the true faith,[6] a Church chosen to everlasting life.[7] And I believe that I am[8] and forever shall remain a living member of it.[9]

[1] John 10:11; Acts 20:28; Eph. 4:11-13; Col. 1:18 [2] Gen. 26:4; Rev. 5:9 [3] Is. 59:21; 1 Cor. 11:26 [4] Ps. 129:1-5; Matt. 16:18; John 10:28-30 [5] Rom. 1:16; 10:14-17; Eph. 5:26 [6] Acts 2:42-47; Eph. 4:1-6 [7] Rom. 8:29; Eph. 1:3-14 [8] 1 John 3:14, 19-21 [9] Ps. 23:6; John 10:27-28; 1 Cor. 1:4-9; 1 Pet. 1:3-5

Q. 55. What do you understand by "the communion of saints"?

A. First, that believers, all and everyone, as members of Christ, have communion with Him and share in all His treasures and gifts.[1] Second, that everyone is duty-bound to use his gifts readily and cheerfully for the benefit and well-being of the other members.[2]

[1] Rom. 8:32; 1 Cor. 6:17; 12:4-7, 12-13; 1 John 1:3 [2] Rom. 12:4-8; 1 Cor. 12:20-27; 13:1-7; Phil. 2:4-8

Q. 56. What do you believe concerning "the forgiveness of sins"?

A. I believe that God, because of Christ's satisfaction, will no more remember my sins[1] nor my sinful nature against which I have to struggle all my life,[2] but He will graciously grant me the righteousness of Christ that I may never come into condemnation.[3]

[1] Ps. 103:3-4, 10, 12; Mic. 7:18-19; 2 Cor. 5:18-21; 1 John 1:7; 2:2 [2] Rom. 7:21-25 [3] John 3:17-18; 5:24; Rom. 8:1–2

LORD'S DAY 22

Q. 57. What comfort does "the resurrection of the body" offer you?

A. Not only shall my soul after this life immediately be taken up to Christ, my Head,[1] but also this my flesh, raised by the power of Christ, shall be reunited with my soul and made like Christ's glorious body.[2]

[1] Luke 16:22; 23:43; Phil. 1:21-23 [2] Job 19:25-26; 1 Cor. 15:20, 42-46, 54; Phil. 3:21; 1 John 3:2

Q. 58. What comfort do you receive from the article about "the life everlasting"?

A. Since I now already feel in my heart the beginning of eternal joy,[1] I shall after this life possess perfect blessedness such as no eye has seen nor ear heard nor the heart of man conceived—a blessedness in which to praise God forever.[2]

[1] John 17:3; Rom. 14:17; 2 Cor. 5:2-3 [2] John 17:24; 1 Cor. 2:9

LORD'S DAY 23

Q. 59. But what does it help you now that you believe all this?

A. In Christ, I am righteous before God and heir to life everlasting.[1]

[1] Hab. 2:4; John 3:36; Rom. 1:17; 5:1-2

Q. 60. How are you righteous before God?

A. Only by true faith in Jesus Christ.[1] Although my conscience accuses me that I have grievously sinned against all God's commandments, have never kept any of them,[2] and am still inclined to all evil,[3] yet God, without any merit of my own,[4] out of mere grace,[5] imputes to me the perfect satisfaction, righteousness, and holiness of Christ.[6] He grants these to me as if I had never had nor committed any sin and as if I myself had accomplished all the obedience which Christ has rendered for me,[7] if only I accept this gift with a believing heart.[8]

[1] Rom. 3:21-28; Gal. 2:16; Eph. 2:8-9; Phil. 3:8-11 [2] Rom. 3:9-10 [3] Rom. 7:23 [4] Deut. 9:6; Ezek. 36:22; Titus 3:4-5 [5] Rom. 3:24; Eph. 2:8 [6] Rom. 4:3-5; 2 Cor. 5:17-19; 1 John 2:1-2 [7] Rom. 4:24-25; 2 Cor. 5:21 [8] John 3:18; Acts 16:30-31; Rom. 3:22

Q. 61. Why do you say that you are righteous only by faith?

A. Not that I am acceptable to God on account of the worthiness of my faith, for only the satisfaction, righteousness, and holiness of Christ is my righteousness before God.[1] I can receive this righteousness and make it my own by faith only.[2]

[1] 1 Cor. 1:30-31; 2:2 [2] Rom. 10:10; 1 John 5:10-12

LORD'S DAY 24

Q. 62. But why can our good works not be our righteousness before God or at least a part of it?

A. Because the righteousness which can stand before God's judgment must be absolutely perfect and in complete agreement with the law of God,[1] whereas even our best works in this life are all imperfect and defiled with sin.[2]

[1] Deut. 27:26; Gal. 3:10 [2] Is. 64:6

Q. 63. But do our good works earn nothing even though God promises to reward them in this life and the next?

A. This reward is not earned[1]; it is a gift of grace.[2]

[1] Matt. 5:12; Heb. 11:6 [2] Luke 17:10; 2 Tim. 4:7-8

Q. 64. Does this teaching not make people careless and wicked?

A. No. It is impossible that those grafted into Christ by true faith should not bring forth fruits of thankfulness.[1]

[1] Matt. 7:18; Luke 6:43-45; John 15:5

LORD'S DAY 25

Q. 65. Since then faith alone makes us share in Christ and all His benefits, where does this faith come from?

A. From the Holy Spirit[1] who works it in our hearts by the preaching of the gospel[2] and strengthens it by the use of the sacraments.[3]

[1] John 3:5; 1 Cor. 2:10-14; Eph. 2:8; Phil. 1:29 [2] Rom. 10:17; 1 Pet. 1:23-25 [3] Matt. 28:19-20; 1 Cor. 10:16

Q. 66. What are the sacraments?

A. The sacraments are holy, visible signs and seals. They were instituted by God so that by their use He might the more fully declare and seal to us the promise of the gospel.[1] And this is the promise: that God graciously grants us forgiveness of sins and everlasting life because of the one sacrifice of Christ accomplished on the cross.[2]

[1] Gen. 17:11; Deut. 30:6; Rom. 4:11 [2] Matt. 26:27-28; Acts 2:38; Heb. 10:10

Q. 67. Are both the Word and the sacraments, then, intended to focus our faith on the sacrifice of Jesus Christ on the cross as the only ground of our salvation?

A. Yes, indeed. The Holy Spirit teaches us in the gospel and assures us by the sacraments that our entire salvation rests on Christ's one sacrifice for us on the cross.[1]

[1] Rom. 6:3; 1 Cor. 11:26; Gal. 3:27

Q. 68. How many sacraments has Christ instituted in the new covenant?

A. Two: holy baptism and the holy supper.[1]

[1] Matt. 28:19-20; 1 Cor. 11:23-26

LORD'S DAY 26

Q. 69. How does holy baptism signify and seal to you that the one sacrifice of Christ on the cross benefits you?

A. In this way: Christ instituted this outward washing[1] and with it gave the promise that, as surely as water washes away the dirt from the body, so certainly His blood and Spirit wash away the impurity of my soul, that is, all my sins.[2]

[1] Matt. 28:19 [2] Matt. 3:11; Mark 16:16; John 1:33; Acts 2:38; Rom. 6:3–4; 1 Pet. 3:21

Q. 70. What does it mean to be washed with Christ's blood and Spirit?

A. To be washed with Christ's blood means to receive forgiveness of sins from God, through grace, because of Christ's blood poured out for us in His sacrifice on the cross.[1] To be washed with His Spirit means to be renewed by the Holy Spirit and sanctified to be members of Christ so that more and more we become dead to sin and lead a holy and blameless life.[2]

[1] Ez. 36:25; Zech. 13:1; Eph. 1:7; Heb. 12:24; 1 Pet. 1:2; Rev. 1:5; 7:14 [2] John 3:5-8; Rom. 6:4; 1 Cor. 6:11; Col. 2:11-12

Q. 71. Where has Christ promised that He will wash us with his blood and Spirit as surely as we are washed with the water of baptism?

A. In the institution of baptism where he says: "*Go therefore and make disciples of all nations, baptizing them in the name of the Father and of the Son and of the Holy Spirit.*"[1] "*He who believes and is baptized will be saved, but he who does not believe will be condemned.*"[2] This promise is repeated where Scripture calls baptism the "*washing of regeneration*"[3] and the washing away of sins.[4]

[1] Matt. 28:19 [2] Mk. 16:16 [3] Titus 3:5 [4] Acts 22:16

LORD'S DAY 27

Q. 72. Does this outward washing with water itself wash away sins?

A. No, only the blood of Jesus Christ and the Holy Spirit cleanse us from all sins.[1]

[1] Matt. 3:11; 1 Pet. 3:21; 1 John 1:7

Q. 73. Why then does the Holy Spirit call baptism the *"washing of regeneration"* and the washing away of sins?

A. God speaks in this way for a good reason. He wants to teach us that the blood and Spirit of Christ remove our sins just as water takes away dirt from the body.[1] But, even more important, He wants to assure us by this divine pledge and sign that we are as truly cleansed from our sins spiritually as we are bodily washed with water.[2]

[1] 1 Cor. 6:11; Rev. 1:5; 7:14 [2] Mark 16:16; Acts 2:38; Rom. 6:3-4; Gal. 3:27

Q. 74. Should infants too be baptized?

A. Yes. Infants as well as adults belong to God's covenant and congregation.[1] Through Christ's blood, the redemption from sin and the Holy Spirit who works faith are promised to them no less than to adults.[2] Therefore, by baptism, as the sign of the covenant, they must be grafted into the Christian church and distinguished from the children of unbelievers.[3] This was done in the old covenant by circumcision,[4] in place of which baptism was instituted in the new covenant.[5]

[1] Gen. 17:7; Matt. 19:14 [2] Ps. 22:10; Is. 44:1-3; Acts 2:38-39; 16:31 [3] Acts 10:47; 1 Cor. 7:14 [4] Gen. 17:9-14 [5] Col. 2:11-13

LORD'S DAY 28

Q. 75. How does the Lord's Supper signify and seal to you that you share in Christ's one sacrifice on the cross and in all His gifts?

A. In this way: Christ has commanded me and all believers to eat of this broken bread and drink of this cup in remembrance of Him. With this command, He gave these promises:[1] First, as surely as I see with my eyes the bread of the Lord broken for me and the cup given to me, so surely was His body offered for me and His blood poured out for me on the cross. Second, as surely as I receive from the hand of the minister and taste with my mouth the bread and the cup of the Lord as sure signs of Christ's body and blood, so surely does He Himself nourish and refresh my soul to everlasting life with His crucified body and shed blood.

[1] Matt. 26:26-28; Mark 14:22-24; Luke 22:19-20; 1 Cor. 11:23-25

Q. 76. What does it mean to eat the crucified body of Christ and to drink His shed blood?

A. First, to accept with a believing heart all the suffering and the death of Christ and so receive forgiveness of sins and life eternal.[1] Second, to be united more and more to His sacred body through the Holy Spirit, who lives both in Christ and in us.[2] Therefore, although Christ is in heaven[3] and we are on earth, yet we are flesh of His flesh and bone of His bones,[4] and we forever live and are governed by one Spirit, as the members of our body are by one soul.[5]

[1] John 6:35, 40, 50-54 [2] John 6:55-56; 1 Cor. 12:13 [3] Acts 1:9-11; 3:21; 1 Cor. 11:26; Col. 3:1 [4] 1 Cor. 6:15, 17; Eph. 5:29-30; 1 John 4:13 [5] John 6:56-58; 15:1-6; Eph. 4:15-16; 1 John 3:24

Q. 77. Where has Christ promised that He will nourish and refresh believers with His body and blood as surely as they eat of this broken bread and drink of this cup?

A. In the institution of the Lord's Supper: "*the Lord Jesus on the night when he was betrayed took bread, and when he had given thanks, he broke it, and said, 'This is my body which is for you. Do this in remembrance of me.' In the same way also the cup, after supper, saying, 'Do this, as often as you drink it, in remembrance of me.' For as often as you eat this bread and drink the cup, you proclaim the Lord's death until he comes.*"[1] This promise is repeated by Paul where he says: "*The cup of blessing which we bless, is it not a participation in the blood of Christ? The bread which we break, is it not a participation in the body of Christ? Because there is one bread, we who are many are one body, for we all partake of the one bread.*"[2]

[1] 1 Cor. 11:23-26 [2] 1 Cor. 10:16-17

LORD'S DAY 29

Q. 78. Are then the bread and wine changed into the real body and blood of Christ?

A. No. Just as the water of baptism is not changed into the blood of Christ and is not the washing away of sins itself but is simply God's sign and pledge,[1] so also the bread in the Lord's Supper does not become the body of Christ itself,[2] although it is called Christ's body[3] in keeping with the nature and usage of sacraments.[4]

[1] Eph. 5:26; Titus 3:5 [2] Matt. 26:26-29 [3] 1 Cor. 10:16-17; 11:26-28 [4] Gen. 17:10-11; Ex. 12:11, 13; 1 Cor. 10:3-4; 1 Pet. 3:21

Q. 79. Why then does Christ call the bread His body and the cup His blood or the new covenant in His blood, and why does Paul speak of a participation in the body and blood of Christ?

A. Christ speaks in this way for a good reason. He wants to teach us by His Supper that as bread and wine sustain us in this temporal life, so His crucified body and shed blood are true food and drink for our souls to eternal life.[1] But even more important, He wants to assure us by this visible sign and pledge, first, that through the working of the Holy Spirit we share in His true body and blood as surely as we receive with our mouth these holy signs in remembrance of him,[2] and, second, that all His suffering and obedience are as certainly ours as if we personally had suffered and paid for our sins.[3]

[1] John 6:51, 55 [2] I Cor. 10:16-17; 11:26 [3] Rom. 6:5-11

LORD'S DAY 30

Q. 80. What difference is there between the Lord's Supper and the papal mass?

A. The Lord's Supper testifies to us, first, that we have complete forgiveness of all our sins through the one sacrifice of Jesus Christ which He Himself accomplished on the cross once for all;[1] and, second, that through the Holy Spirit we are grafted into Christ,[2] who with His true body is now in heaven at the right hand of the Father,[3] and this is where He wants to be worshiped.[4] But the mass teaches, first, that the living and the dead do not have forgiveness of sins through the suffering of Christ unless He is still offered for them daily by the priests; and, second, that Christ is bodily present in the form of bread and wine, and there is to be worshiped. Therefore, the mass is basically nothing but a denial of the one sacrifice and suffering of Jesus Christ and an accursed idolatry.

[1] Matt. 26:28; John 19:30; Heb. 7:27; 9:12, 25-26; 10:10-18 [2] 1 Cor. 6:17; 10:16-17 [3] John 20:17; Acts 7:55-56; Heb. 1:3; 8:1 [4] John 4:21-24; Phil. 3:20; Col. 3:1; 1 Thess. 1:10

Q. 81. Who are to come to the table of the Lord?

A. Those who are truly displeased with themselves because of their sins and yet trust that these are forgiven them and that their remaining weakness is covered by the suffering and death of Christ, and who also desire more and more to strengthen their faith and amend their life. But hypocrites and those who do not repent eat and drink judgment upon themselves.[1]

[1] 1 Cor. 10:19-22; 11:26-32

Q. 82. Are those also to be admitted to the Lord's Supper who by their confession and life show that they are unbelieving and ungodly?

A. No, for then the covenant of God would be profaned and His wrath kindled against the whole congregation.[1] Therefore, according to the command of Christ and His apostles, the Christian church is duty-bound to exclude such persons by the keys of the kingdom of heaven until they amend their lives.

[1] Ps. 50:16; Is. 1:11-17; 1 Cor. 11:17-34

LORD'S DAY 31

Q. 83. What are the keys of the kingdom of heaven?

A. The preaching of the holy gospel and church discipline. By these two the kingdom of heaven is opened to believers and closed to unbelievers.[1]

[1] Matt. 16:19; John 20:21-23

Q. 84. How is the kingdom of heaven opened and closed by the preaching of the gospel?

A. According to the command of Christ, the kingdom of heaven is opened when it is proclaimed and publicly testified to every believer that God has really forgiven all their sins for the sake of Christ's merits as often as they by true faith accept the promise of the gospel. The kingdom of heaven is closed when it is proclaimed and testified to all unbelievers and hypocrites that the wrath of God and eternal condemnation rest on them as long as they do not repent. According to this testimony of the gospel, God will judge both in this life and in the life to come.[1]

[1] Matt. 16:19; John 3:31-36; 20:21-23

Q. 85. How is the kingdom of heaven closed and opened by church discipline?

A. According to the command of Christ, people who call themselves Christians but show themselves to be unchristian in doctrine or life are first repeatedly admonished in a brotherly manner. If they do not give up their errors or wickedness, they are reported to the church, that is, to the elders. If they do not heed also their admonitions, they are forbidden the use of the sacraments, and they are excluded by the elders from the Christian congregation and by God himself from the kingdom of Christ.[1] They are again received as members of Christ and of the church when they promise and show real amendment.[2]

[1] Matt. 18:15-20; 1 Cor. 5:3-5; 11-13; 2 Thess. 3:14-15 [2] Luke 15:20-24; 2 Cor. 2:6-11

GRATITUDE: YOUR CHRISTIAN LIFE

LORD'S DAY 32

Q. 86. Since we have been delivered from our misery by grace alone through Christ, without any merit of our own, why must we yet do good works?

A. Because Christ, having redeemed us by His blood, also renews us by His Holy Spirit to be His image, so that with our whole life we may show ourselves thankful to God for His benefits,[1] and He may be praised by us.[2] Further, that we ourselves may be assured of our faith by its fruits,[3] and that by our godly walk of life, we may win our neighbors for Christ.[4]

[1] Rom. 6:13; 12:1-2; 1 Pet. 2:5-10 [2] Matt. 5:16; 1 Cor. 6:19-20 [3] Matt. 7:17-18; Gal. 5:22-24; 2 Pet. 1:10-11 [4] Matt. 5:14-16; Rom. 14:17-19; 1 Pet. 2:12; 3:1-2

Q. 87. Can those be saved who do not turn to God from their ungrateful and impenitent walk of life?

A. By no means. Scripture says that no unchaste person, idolater, adulterer, thief, greedy person, drunkard, slanderer, robber, or the like shall inherit the kingdom of God.[1]

[1] 1 Cor. 6:9-10; Gal. 5:19-21; Eph. 5:5-6; 1 John 3:14

LORD'S DAY 33

Q. 88. What is the true repentance or conversion of man?

A. It is the dying of the old nature and the coming to life of the new.[1]

[1] Rom. 6:1-11; 1 Cor. 5:7; 2 Cor. 5:17; Eph. 4:22-24; Col. 3:5-10

Q. 89. What is the dying of the old nature?

A. It is to grieve with heartfelt sorrow that we have offended God by our sin and more and more to hate it and flee from it.[1]

[1] Ps. 51:3-4, 17; Joel 2:12-13; Rom. 8:12-13; 2 Cor. 7:10

Q. 90. What is the coming to life of the new nature?

A. It is a heartfelt joy in God through Christ[1] and a love and delight to live according to the will of God in all good works.[2]

[1] Ps. 51:8, 12; Is. 57:15; Rom. 5:1; 14:17 [2] Rom. 6:10-11; Gal. 2:20

Q. 91. But what are good works?

A. Only those which are done out of true faith,[1] in accordance with the law of God,[2] and to His glory,[3] and not those based on our own opinion or on precepts of men.[4]

[1] John 15:5; Rom. 14:23; Heb. 11:6 [2] Lev. 18:4; 1 Sam. 15:22; Eph. 2:10 [3] I Cor. 10:31 [4] Deut. 12:32; Is. 29:13; Ezek. 20:18-19; Matt. 15:7-9

LORD'S DAY 34

Q. 92. What is the law of the LORD?

A. "God spoke all these words, saying, 'I am the LORD your God, who brought you out of the land of Egypt, out of the house of bondage. [1] You shall have no other gods before me. [2] You shall not make for yourself a carved image, or any likeness of anything that is in heaven above, or that is in the earth beneath, or that is in the water under the earth. You shall not bow down to them or serve them, for I the LORD your God am a jealous God, visiting the iniquity of the fathers on the children to the third and fourth generation of those who hate me, but showing steadfast love to thousands of those who love me and keep my commandments. [3] You shall not take the name of the LORD your God in vain, for the LORD will not hold him guiltless who takes his name in vain. [4] Remember the Sabbath day, to keep it holy. Six days you shall labor, and do all your work, but the seventh day is a Sabbath to the LORD your God. On it you shall not do any work, you, or your son, or your daughter, your male servant, or your female servant, or your livestock, or the sojourner who is within your gates. For in six days the LORD made heaven and earth, the sea, and all that is in them, and rested the seventh day. Therefore the LORD blessed the Sabbath day and made it holy. [5] Honor your father and your mother, that your days may be long in the land that the LORD your God is giving you. [6] You shall not murder. [7] You shall not commit adultery. [8] You shall not steal. [9] You shall not bear false witness against your neighbor. [10] You shall not covet your neighbor's house; you shall not covet your neighbor's wife, or his male servant, or his female servant, or his ox, or his donkey, or anything that is your neighbor's.'"1

1 Ex. 20:1-17; Deut. 5:6-21

Q. 93. How are these commandments divided?

A. Into two parts. The first teaches us how to live in relation to God; the second, what duties we owe our neighbor.1

1 Matt. 22:37-40

Q. 94. What does the LORD require in the first commandment?

A. That, for the sake of my very salvation, I avoid and flee all idolatry,1 witchcraft, superstition,2 and prayer to saints or to other creatures.3 Further, that I rightly come to know the only true God,4 trust in Him alone,5 submit to Him with all humility6 and patience,7 expect all good from Him only,8 and love,9 fear,10 and honor Him11 with all my heart. In short, that I forsake all creatures rather than do the least thing against His will.12

1 1 Cor. 6:9-10; 10:5-14; 1 John 5:21 2 Lev. 19:31; Deut. 18:9-12 3 Matt. 4:10; Rev. 19:10; 22:8-9 4 John 17:3 5 Jer. 17:5, 7 6 1 Pet. 5:5-6 7 Rom. 5:3-4; 1 Cor. 10:10; Phil. 2:14; Col. 1:11; Heb. 10:36 8 Ps. 104:27-28; Is. 45:7; James 1:17 9 Deut. 6:5; Matt. 22:37 10 Deut. 6:2; Ps. 111:10; Prov. 1:7; 9:10; Matt. 10:28; 1 Pet. 1:17 11 Deut. 6:13; Matt. 4:10; Deut. 10:20 12 Matt. 5:29-30; 10:37-39; Acts 5:29

Q. 95. What is idolatry?

A. Idolatry is having or inventing something in which to put our trust instead of, or in addition to, the only true God who has revealed Himself in His Word.[1]

[1] 1 Chron. 16:26; Gal. 4:8-9; Eph. 5:5; Phil. 3:19

LORD'S DAY 35

Q. 96. What does God require in the second commandment?

A. We are not to make an image of God in any way[1] nor to worship Him in any other manner than He has commanded in his Word.[2]

[1] Deut. 4:15-19; Is. 40:18-25; Acts 17:29; Rom. 1:23 [2] Lev. 10:1-7; Deut. 12:30; 1 Sam. 15:22-23; Matt. 15:9; John 4:23-24

Q. 97. May we then not make any image at all?

A. God cannot and may not be visibly portrayed in any way. Creatures may be portrayed, but God forbids us to make or have any images of them in order to worship them or to serve God through them.[1]

[1] Ex. 34:13-14, 17; Num. 33:52; 2 Kings 18:4-5; Is. 40:25

Q. 98. But may images not be tolerated in the churches as "books for the laity"?

A. No, for we should not be wiser than God. He wants His people to be taught, not by means of speechless images[1] but by the living preaching of His Word.[2]

[1] Jer. 10:8; Hab. 2:18-20 [2] Rom. 10:14-15, 17; 2 Tim. 3:16-17; 2 Pet. 1:19

LORD'S DAY 36

Q. 99. What is required in the third commandment?

A. We are not to blaspheme or to abuse the Name of God by cursing,[1] perjury,[2] or unnecessary oaths,[3] nor to share in such horrible sins by being silent bystanders.[4] In short, we must use the holy Name of God only with fear and reverence,[5] so that we may rightly confess Him,[6] call upon Him,[7] and praise Him in all our words and works.[8]

[1] Lev. 24:10-17 [2] Lev. 19:12 [3] Matt. 5:37; James 5:12 [4] Lev. 5:1; Prov. 29:24 [5] Ps. 99:1-5; Is. 45:23; Jer. 4:2 [6] Matt. 10:32-33; Rom. 10:9-10 [7] Ps. 50:14-15; 1 Tim. 2:8 [8] Rom. 2:24; Col. 3:17; 1 Tim. 6:1

Q. 100. Is the blaspheming of God's Name by swearing and cursing such a grievous sin that God is angry also with those who do not prevent and forbid it as much as they can?

A. Certainly,[1] for no sin is greater or provokes God's wrath more than the blaspheming of His Name. That is why He commanded it to be punished with death.[2]

[1] Lev. 5:1 [2] Lev. 24:16

LORD'S DAY 37

Q. 101. But may we swear an oath by the Name of God in a godly manner?

A. Yes, when the government demands it of its subjects, or when necessity requires it, in order to maintain and promote fidelity and truth to God's glory and for our neighbor's good. Such oath-taking is based on God's Word[1] and was therefore rightly used by saints in the Old and the New Testament.[2]

[1] Deut. 6:13; 10:20; Jer. 4:1-2; Heb. 6:16 [2] Gen. 21:24; 31:53; Josh. 9:15; 1 Sam. 24:22; 1 Kings 1:29-30; Rom. 1:9; 2 Cor. 1:23

Q. 102. May we also swear by saints or other creatures?

A. No. A lawful oath is a calling upon God, who alone knows the heart, to bear witness to the truth and to punish me if I swear falsely.[1] No creature is worthy of such honor.[2]

[1] Rom. 9:1; 2 Cor. 1:23 [2] Matt. 5:34-37; 23:16-22; James 5:12

LORD'S DAY 38

Q. 103. What does God require in the fourth commandment?

A. First, that the ministry of the gospel and the schools be maintained[1] and that, especially on the day of rest, I diligently attend the church of God[2] to hear God's Word,[3] to use the sacraments,[4] to call publicly upon the LORD,[5] and to give Christian offerings for the poor.[6] Second, that all the days of my life I rest from my evil works, let the LORD work in me through His Holy Spirit, and so begin in this life the eternal sabbath.[7]

[1] Deut. 6:4-9, 20-25; 1 Cor. 9:13-14; 2 Tim. 2:2; 3:13-17; Titus 1:5 [2] Deut. 12:5-12; Ps. 40:9-10; 68:26; Acts 2:42-47; Heb. 10:23-25 [3] Rom. 10:14-17; 1 Cor. 14:26-33; 1 Tim. 4:13 [4] 1 Cor. 11:23-24 [5] Col. 3:16; 1 Tim. 2:1 [6] Ps. 50:14; 1 Cor. 16:2; 2 Cor. 8 and 9 [7] Is. 66:23; Heb. 4:9-11

LORD'S DAY 39

Q. 104. What does God require in the fifth commandment?

A. That I show all honor, love, and faithfulness to my father and mother and to all those in authority over me, submit myself with due obedience to their good instruction and discipline,[1] and also have patience with their weaknesses and shortcomings,[2] since it is God's will to govern us by their hand.[3]

[1] Ex. 21:17; Prov. 1:8; 4:1; Rom. 13:1-2; Eph. 5:21-22; 6:1-9; Col. 3:18-4:1 [2] Prov. 20:20; 23:22; 1 Pet. 2:18 [3] Matt. 22:21; Rom. 13:1-8; Eph. 6:1-9; Col. 3:18-21

LORD'S DAY 40

Q. 105. What does God require in the sixth commandment?

A. I am not to dishonor, hate, injure, or kill my neighbor by thoughts, words, or gestures, and much less by deeds, whether personally or through another;[1] rather, I am to put away all desire of revenge.[2] Moreover, I am not to harm or recklessly endanger myself.[3] Therefore, also, the government bears the sword to prevent murder.[4]

[1] Gen. 9:6; Lev. 19:17-18; Matt. 5:21-22; 26:52 [2] Prov. 25:21–22; Matt. 18:35; Rom. 12:19; Eph. 4:26 [3] Matt. 4:7; 26:52; Rom. 13:11-14 [4] Gen. 9:6; Ex. 21:14; Rom. 13:4

Q. 106. But does this commandment speak only of killing?

A. By forbidding murder, God teaches us that He hates the root of murder, such as envy, hatred, anger, and desire of revenge,[1] and that He regards all these as murder.[2]

[1] Prov. 14:30; Rom. 1:29; 12:19; Gal. 5:19-21; James 1:20; 1 John 2:9-11 [2] 1 John 3:15

Q. 107. Is it enough, then, that we do not kill our neighbor in any such way?

A. No. When God condemns envy, hatred, and anger, he commands us to love our neighbor as ourselves,[1] to show patience, peace, gentleness, mercy, and friendliness toward him,[2] to protect him from harm as much as we can, and to do good even to our enemies.[3]

[1] Matt. 7:12; 22:39; Rom. 12:10 [2] Matt. 5:5; Luke 6:36; Rom. 12:10, 18; Gal. 6:1-2; Eph. 4:2; Col. 3:12; 1 Pet. 3:8 [3] Ex. 23:4-5; Matt. 5:44-45; Rom. 12:20

LORD'S DAY 41

Q. 108. What does the seventh commandment teach us?

A. That all unchastity is cursed by God.[1] We must therefore detest it from the heart[2] and live chaste and disciplined lives both inside and outside of holy marriage.[3]

[1] Lev. 18:30; Eph. 5:3-5 [2] Jude 22-23 [3] 1 Cor. 7:1-9; 1 Thess. 4:3-8; Heb. 13:4

Q. 109. Does God in this commandment forbid nothing more than adultery and similar shameful sins?

A. Since we, body and soul, are temples of the Holy Spirit, it is God's will that we keep ourselves pure and holy. Therefore, He forbids all unchaste acts, gestures, words, thoughts, desires,[2] and whatever may entice us to unchastity.[3]

[1] Matt. 5:27-29; 1 Cor. 6:18-20; Eph. 5:3-4 [2] 1 Cor. 15:33; Eph. 5:18

LORD'S DAY 42

Q. 110. What does God forbid in the eighth commandment?

A. God forbids not only outright theft and robbery[1] but also such wicked schemes and devices as false weights and measures, deceptive merchandising, counterfeit money, and usury;[2] we must not defraud our neighbor in any way, whether by force or by show of right.[3] In addition, God forbids all greed[4] and all abuse or squandering of His gifts.[5]

[1] Ex. 22:1; 1 Cor. 5:9-10; 6:9-10 [2] Deut. 25:13-16; Ps. 15:5; Prov. 11:1; 12:22; Ezek. 45:9-12; Luke 6:35 [3] Mic. 6:9-11; Luke 3:14; James 5:1-6 [4] Luke 12:15; Eph. 5:5 [5] Prov. 21:20; 23:20-21; Luke 16:10-13

Q. 111. What does God require of you in this commandment?

A. I must promote my neighbor's good wherever I can and may, deal with him as I would like others to deal with me, and work faithfully so that I may be able to give to those in need.[1]

[1] Is. 58:5-10; Matt. 7:12; Gal. 6:9-10; Eph. 4:28

LORD'S DAY 43

Q. 112. What is required in the ninth commandment?

A. I must not give false testimony against anyone, twist no one's words, not gossip or slander, nor condemn or join in condemning anyone rashly and unheard.[1] Rather, I must avoid all lying and deceit as the devil's own works under penalty of God's heavy wrath.[2] In court and everywhere else, I must love the truth,[3] speak and confess it honestly, and do what I can to defend and promote my neighbor's honor and reputation.[4]

[1] Ps. 15; Prov. 19:5, 9; 21:28; Matt. 7:1; Luke 6:37; Rom. 1:28-32 [2] Lev. 19:11-12; Prov. 12:22; 13:5; John 8:44; Rev. 21:8 [3] 1 Cor. 13:6; Eph. 4:25 [4] 1 Pet. 3:8-9; 4:8

LORD'S DAY 44

Q. 113. What does the tenth commandment require of us?

A. That not even the slightest thought or desire contrary to any of God's commandments should ever arise in our heart. Rather, we should always hate all sin with all our heart and delight in all righteousness.[1]

[1] Ps. 19:7-14; 139:23-24; Rom. 7:7-8

Q. 114. But can those converted to God keep these commandments perfectly?

A. No. In this life even the holiest have only a small beginning of this obedience.[1] Nevertheless, with earnest purpose, they do begin to live not only according to some but to all the commandments of God.[2]

[1] Eccles. 7:20; Rom. 7:14-15; 1 Cor. 13:9; 1 John 1:8 [2] Ps. 1:1-2; Rom. 7:22-25; Phil. 3:12-16

Q. 115. If in this life no one can keep the Ten Commandments perfectly, why does God have them preached so strictly?

A. First, that throughout our life we may more and more become aware of our sinful nature and therefore seek more eagerly the forgiveness of sins and righteousness in Christ.[1] Second, that we may be zealous for good deeds and constantly pray to God for the grace of the Holy Spirit that He may more and more renew us after God's image until after this life we reach the goal of perfection.[2]

[1] Ps. 32:5; Rom. 3:19-26; 7:7, 24-25; 1 John 1:9 [2] 1 Cor. 9:24; Phil. 3:12-14; 1 John 3:1-3

LORD'S DAY 45

Q. 116. Why is prayer necessary for Christians?

A. Because prayer is the most important part of the thankfulness which God requires of us.[1] Moreover, God will give His grace and the Holy Spirit only to those who constantly and with heartfelt longing ask Him for these gifts and thank Him for them.[2]

[1] Ps. 50:14-15; 116:12-19; 1 Thess. 5:16-18 [2] Matt. 7:7-8; Luke 11:9-13

Q. 117. What belongs to a prayer which pleases God and is heard by Him?

A. First, we must from the heart call upon the one true God only, who has revealed Himself in His Word, for all that He has commanded us to pray.[1] Second, we must thoroughly know our need and misery, so that we may humble ourselves before God.[2] Third, we must rest on this firm foundation that, although we do not deserve it, God will certainly hear our prayer for the sake of Christ our Lord, as He has promised us in his Word.[3]

[1] Ps. 145:18-20; John 4:22-24; Rom. 8:26-27; James 1:5; 1 John 5:14-15; Rev. 19:10
[2] 2 Chron. 7:14; 20:12; Ps. 2:11; 34:18; 62:8; Is. 66:2; Rev. 4 [3] Dan. 9:17-19; Matt. 7:8; John 14:13-14; 16:23; Rom. 10:13; James 1:6

Q. 118. What has God commanded us to ask of Him?

A. All the things we need for body and soul[1] as included in the prayer which Christ our Lord himself taught us.

[1] Matt. 6:33; James 1:17

Q. 119. What is the Lord's Prayer?

A. "*Our Father who art in heaven, hallowed be Thy Name. Thy kingdom come, Thy will be done, on earth as it is in heaven. Give us this day our daily bread, and forgive us our debts, as we also have forgiven our debtors. And lead us not into temptation, but deliver us from the evil one. [For Thine is the kingdom and the power and the glory, forever. Amen.]*"[1]

[1] Matt. 6:9-13; Luke 11:2-4; early manuscripts of the Bible do not include the bracketed words.

LORD'S DAY 46

Q. 120. Why has Christ commanded us to address God as "*Our Father*"?

A. To awaken in us at the very beginning of our prayer that childlike reverence and trust toward God which should be basic to our prayer: God has become our Father through Christ and will much less deny us what we ask of Him in faith than our fathers would refuse us earthly things.[1]

[1] Matt. 7:9-11; Luke 11:11-13

Q. 121. Why is there added, "*who art in heaven*"?

A. These words teach us not to think of God's heavenly majesty in an earthly manner[1] and to expect from His almighty power all things we need for body and soul.[2]

[1] Jer.23:23-24; Acts 17:24-25 [2] Mt.6:25-34; Rom.8:31-32

LORD'S DAY 47

Q. 122. What is the first petition?

A. "*Hallowed be Thy Name.*" That is: Grant us, first of all, that we may rightly know You[1] and sanctify, glorify, and praise You in all Your works in which shine forth Your almighty power, wisdom, goodness, righteousness, mercy, and truth.[2] Grant us also that we may so direct our whole life—our thoughts, words, and actions—that Your name is not blasphemed because of us but always honored and praised.[3]

[1] Jer. 9:23-24; 31:33-34; Matt. 16:17; John 17:3 [2] Ex. 34:5-8; Ps. 145; Jer. 32:16-20; Luke 1:46-55, 68-75; Rom. 11:33-36 [3] Ps. 115:1; Matt. 5:16

LORD'S DAY 48

Q. 123. What is the second petition?

A. "*Thy kingdom come.*" That is: So rule us by Your Word and Spirit that more and more we submit to You.[1] Preserve and increase Your church.[2] Destroy the works of the devil, every power that raises itself against You, and every conspiracy against Your holy Word.[3] Do all this until the fullness of Your kingdom comes, wherein You shall be all in all.[4]

[1] Ps. 119:5, 105; 143:10; Matt. 6:33 [2] Ps. 51:18; 122:6-9; Matt. 16:18; Acts 2:42-47 [3] Rom. 16:20; 1 John 3:8 [4] Rom. 8:22-23; 1 Cor. 15:28; Rev. 22: 17, 20

LORD'S DAY 49

Q. 124. What is the third petition?

A. "*Thy will be done, on earth as it is in heaven.*" That is: Grant that we and all men may deny our own will, and without any murmuring, obey Your will, for it alone is good.[1] Grant also that everyone may carry out the duties of his office and calling[2] as willingly and faithfully as the angels in heaven.[3]

[1] Matt. 7:21; 16:24-26; Luke 22:42; Rom. 12:1-2; Titus 2:11-12 [2] 1 Cor. 7:17-24; Eph. 6:5-9 [3] Ps. 103:20-21

LORD'S DAY 50

Q. 125. What is the fourth petition?

A. *"Give us this day our daily bread."* That is: Provide us with all our bodily needs[1] so that we may acknowledge that You are the only fountain of all good,[2] and that our care and labor and also Your gifts cannot do us any good without Your blessing.[3] Grant, therefore, that we may withdraw our trust from all creatures and place it only in You.[4]

[1] Ps. 104:27-30; 145:15-16; Matt. 6:25-34 [2] Acts 14:17; 17:25; James 1:17 [3] Deut. 8:3; Ps. 37:16; 127:1-2; 1 Cor. 15:58 [4] Ps. 55:22; 62; 146; Jer. 17:5-8; Heb. 13:5-6

LORD'S DAY 51

Q. 126. What is the fifth petition?

A. *"And forgive us our debts, as we also have forgiven our debtors."* That is: For the sake of Christ's blood, do not impute to us, wretched sinners, any of our transgressions nor the evil which still clings to us[1] as we also find this evidence of your grace in us that we are fully determined wholeheartedly to forgive our neighbor.[2]

[1] Ps. 51:1-7; 143:2; Rom. 8:1; 1 John 2:1-2 [2] Matt. 6:14-15; 18:21-35

LORD'S DAY 52

Q. 127. What is the sixth petition?

A. *"And lead us not into temptation, but deliver us from the evil one."* That is: In ourselves, we are so weak that we cannot stand even for a moment.[1] Moreover, our sworn enemies—the devil,[2] the world,[3] and our own flesh[4]—do not cease to attack us. Will You, therefore, uphold and strengthen us by the power of Your Holy Spirit, so that in this spiritual war,[5] we may not go down to defeat but always firmly resist our enemies until we finally obtain the complete victory.[6]

[1] Ps. 103:14-16; John 15:1-5 [2] 2 Cor. 11:14; Eph. 6:10-13; 1 Pet. 5:8 [3] John 15:18-21 [4] Rom. 7:23; Gal. 5:17 [5] Matt. 10:19-20; 26:41; Mark 13:33; Rom. 5:3-5 [6] 1 Cor. 10:13; 1 Thess. 3:13; 5:23

Q. 128. How do you conclude your prayer?

A. "*For Thine is the kingdom and the power and the glory, forever.*" That is: All this we ask of You, because, as our King having power over all things, You are both willing and able to give us all that is good,[1] and because not we but your holy name should so receive all glory forever.[2]

[1] Rom. 10:11-13; 2 Pet 2:9 [2] Ps. 115:1; Jer. 33:8-9; John 14:13

Q. 129. What does the word "*Amen*" mean?

A. "*Amen*" means: It is true and certain. For God has much more certainly heard my prayer than I feel in my heart that I desire this of Him.[1]

[1] Is. 65:24; 2 Cor. 1:20; 2 Tim. 2:13

THREE HISTORIC CHRISTIAN CREEDS

THE APOSTLES' CREED

I believe in God the Father Almighty, Maker of heaven and earth.

And in Jesus Christ, his only begotten Son, our Lord; who was conceived by the Holy Spirit, born of the virgin Mary; suffered under Pontius Pilate; was crucified, dead, and buried; he descended into hell[1]; the third day he arose from the dead; he ascended into heaven, and sits at the right hand of God the Father Almighty; from there he shall come to judge the living and the dead.

I believe in the Holy Spirit; the holy catholic Church[2]; the communion of saints; the forgiveness of sins; the resurrection of the body; and the life everlasting.

[1] Meaning as true man, Jesus fully suffered, in body and soul, the pain and torment of hell on the cross and earlier. See *Heidelberg Catechism* Q&A 44 and the *Canons of Dort* 2.4. [2] Meaning universal church. That is, there is one church across all times, places, and peoples. This does not refer to the Roman Catholic Church.

THE NICENE CREED

I believe in one God, the Father Almighty, Maker of heaven and earth, and of all things visible and invisible.

And in one Lord Jesus Christ, the only begotten Son of God, begotten of the Father before all worlds; God of God, Light of

Light, very God of very God; begotten, not made, being of one substance with the Father, by whom all things were made. Who, for us men and for our salvation, came down from heaven, and was incarnate by the Holy Spirit of the virgin Mary, and was made man; and was crucified also for us under Pontius Pilate; he suffered and was buried; and the third day he rose again, according to the Scriptures; and ascended into heaven, and sits on the right hand of the Father; and he shall come again, with glory, to judge the living and the dead; whose kingdom shall have no end.

And I believe in the Holy Spirit, the Lord and Giver of Life; who proceeds from the Father and the Son; who with the Father and the Son together is worshiped and glorified; who spoke by the prophets. And I believe in one holy catholic[1] and apostolic Church. I acknowledge one baptism for the remission of sins; and I look for the resurrection of the dead, and the life of the world to come. Amen.

[1] See note *two* for the Apostles' Creed.

THE ATHANASIAN CREED

[1] Whoever desires to be saved should above all hold to the catholic[1] faith. [2] Anyone who does not keep it whole and unbroken will doubtless perish eternally.

[3] Now this is the catholic faith: that we worship one God in Trinity and the Trinity in unity, [4] neither confounding their persons nor dividing the essence. [5] For the person of the Father is a distinct person, the person of the Son is another, and that of the Holy Spirit still another. [6] But the divinity of the Father, Son, and Holy Spirit is one, the glory equal, the majesty coeternal. [7] Such as the Father is, such is the Son and

such is the Holy Spirit. [8] The Father is uncreated, the Son is uncreated, the Holy Spirit is uncreated. [9] The Father is immeasurable, the Son is immeasurable, the Holy Spirit is immeasurable. [10] The Father is eternal, the Son is eternal, the Holy Spirit is eternal. [11] And yet there are not three eternal beings; there is but one eternal being. [12] So too there are not three uncreated or immeasurable beings; there is but one uncreated and immeasurable being. [13] Similarly, the Father is almighty, the Son is almighty, the Holy Spirit is almighty. [14] Yet there are not three almighty beings; there is but one almighty being. [15] Thus, the Father is God, the Son is God, the Holy Spirit is God. [16] Yet there are not three gods; there is but one God. [17] Thus, the Father is Lord, the Son is Lord, the Holy Spirit is Lord. [18] Yet there are not three lords; there is but one Lord. [19] Just as Christian truth compels us to confess each person individually as both God and Lord, [20] so catholic religion forbids us to say that there are three gods or lords. [21] The Father was neither made nor created nor begotten from anyone. [22] The Son was neither made nor created; he was begotten from the Father alone. [23] The Holy Spirit was neither made nor created nor begotten; he proceeds from the Father and the Son. [24] Accordingly, there is one Father, not three fathers; there is one Son, not three sons; there is one Holy Spirit, not three holy spirits. [25] None in this Trinity is before or after, none is greater or smaller; [26] in their entirety the three persons are coeternal and coequal with each other. [27] So in everything, as was said earlier, the unity in Trinity, and the Trinity in unity, is to be worshiped. [28] Anyone then who desires to be saved should think thus about the Trinity.

[29] But it is necessary for eternal salvation that one also believe in the incarnation of our Lord Jesus Christ faithfully. [30] Now this is the true faith: that we believe and confess that our Lord Jesus Christ, God's Son, is both God and man, equally. [31] He is God from the essence of the Father, begotten before time; and he is man from the essence of his mother, born in time; [32]

completely God, completely man, with a rational soul and human flesh; [33] equal to the Father as regards divinity, less than the Father as regards humanity. [34] Although he is God and man, yet Christ is not two, but one. [35] He is one, however, not by his divinity being turned into flesh, but by God's taking humanity to himself. [36] He is one, certainly not by the blending of his essence, but by the unity of his person. [37] For just as one man is both rational soul and flesh, so too the one Christ is both God and man. [38] He suffered for our salvation; he descended to hell[2]; he arose from the dead on the third day; [39] he ascended to heaven; he is seated at the Father's right hand; [40] from there he will come to judge the living and the dead. [41] At his coming all people will arise bodily [42] and give an accounting of their own deeds. [43] Those who have done good will enter eternal life, and those who have done evil will enter eternal fire.

[44] This is the catholic faith: that one cannot be saved without believing it firmly and faithfully.

[1] See note *two* for the Apostles' Creed. [2] See note *one* for the Apostles' Creed

ABOUT SMALL TOWN THEOLOGIAN

Small Town Theologian was created by Jonathan L. Shirk to help his local church (jerusalemchurch.net) and other ordinary Christians find deeper comfort and joy in the gospel from a historically Reformed perspective. Small Town Theologian focuses on three things: short books, a weekly podcast, and a blog—**smalltowntheologian.org**.

Jonathan L. Shirk is the pastor of Jerusalem Church, a historic independent Reformed church (est. ~ 1727) in the small town of Manheim, PA. He has degrees from Grove City College (B.S. Marketing Management; 2001) and Reformed Presbyterian Theological Seminary (M.Div.; 2006). He previously served the body of Christ for seven years at North Park Church in Wexford, PA as the Director of Student Ministry.

Jonathan is happily married to his beautiful wife Kristina, and together they enjoy life in a small town with their four children. He is a Pittsburgh Steelers fan and enjoys running, basketball, fly fishing, grilling, hip hop, and much more.

Email Jonathan:
smalltowntheologian@gmail.com

Connect on Facebook:
facebook.com/SmallTownTheologian

Made in the USA
Columbia, SC
11 November 2024